现代经济金融理论与方法／前／沿／研／究／丛／书／

本书获得中央高校基本科研业务费和华中科技大
（项目批准号：2019kfyXJJS101、2020WKYXC

Labor Supply in Urban China
中国城镇居民的劳动供给研究

陈 茜／著

中国财经出版传媒集团
经济科学出版社
Economic Science Press

图书在版编目（CIP）数据

中国城镇居民的劳动供给研究 = Labor Supply in Urban China/陈茜著. --北京：经济科学出版社，2021.12

（现代经济金融理论与方法前沿研究丛书）

ISBN 978-7-5218-3298-3

Ⅰ.①中… Ⅱ.①陈… Ⅲ.①城镇-劳动力调配-研究-中国 Ⅳ.①F249.21

中国版本图书馆 CIP 数据核字（2021）第 255849 号

责任编辑：纪小小
责任校对：徐　昕
责任印制：范　艳

中国城镇居民的劳动供给研究
（Labor Supply in Urban China）
陈　茜　著
经济科学出版社出版、发行　新华书店经销
社址：北京市海淀区阜成路甲 28 号　邮编：100142
总编部电话：010-88191217　发行部电话：010-88191522
网址：www.esp.com.cn
电子邮箱：esp@esp.com.cn
天猫网店：经济科学出版社旗舰店
网址：http://jjkxcbs.tmall.com
北京密兴印刷有限公司印装
710×1000　16 开　8.25 印张　135000 字
2022 年 11 月第 1 版　2022 年 11 月第 1 次印刷
ISBN 978-7-5218-3298-3　定价：38.00 元
（图书出现印装问题，本社负责调换。电话：010-88191510）
（版权所有　侵权必究　打击盗版　举报热线：010-88191661
QQ：2242791300　营销中心电话：010-88191537
电子邮箱：dbts@esp.com.cn）

Preface

This book consists of three essays studying the determination and evolution of labor supply in China. The analysis especially focuses on the labor market behavior of the wage workers with urban registration (*Hukou*). The first chapter outlines the book by briefly discussing the motivations, methods, and main findings in each of the following chapters.

Chapter 2 examines the evolution of female labor supply in urban China. Female labor force participation rate in China has been declining rapidly since the 1990s. Using a time series of cross-sections from the Chinese Household Income Project Series (CHIPS), this chapter attempts to systematically relate the decrease in female labor force participation to the socio-economic changes happening in China during the same period, and assess their respective contributions. Adopting both linear and non-linear decomposition techniques, the results show that during 1988 – 1995, changes in population age distribution and family size both contribute, during 1995 – 2002, age effect dominates, and during 2002 – 2007, non-labor income effect dominates in explaining the decreasing trend in female labor force participation.

Chapter 3 investigates the impact of social norms on married women's labor supply decision in China. Using data from the China General Social Survey (CGSS) and the China Family Panel Studies (CFPS), I find a strong and robust positive correlation between the labor supply behavior of a married woman and the former work experience of her mother-in-law. The estimation results indicate that being raised by a working mother influences both a man's attitude toward gender roles and his household productivity, and therefore married women whose mothers-in-law were not working are themselves significantly less likely to participate in the labor force.

The last chapter evaluates the labor market consequence of rural-to-urban migration in China. Starting from the mid – 1990s, there is a remarkable increase in the number of migrant workers in cities, from around 39 million in 1997 to 145 million by 2009 (Meng et al., 2013). Chapter 4 intends to explore how does this important economic event affect the labor market conditions of urban residents. Specifically, I estimate the possible employment and earnings displacement effects of rural-to-urban migration on urban residents by exploiting regional variation in the rural migrant share of education-experience cells. I use multiple sets of instrumental variable to address the potential endogeneity problems associated with the rural migrant ratio in a city. The estimation results are consistent with the predictions of the textbook model of a competitive labor market, indicating the inflow of rural migrants reduces the wage and labor supply of competing urban residents.

Contents

Chapter 1 Introduction 1

Chapter 2 The Evolution of Female Labor Force Participation in Urban China 6

2.1 Introduction / 6
2.2 Literature Review / 9
2.3 Data and Descriptive Patterns / 14
2.4 Estimation of the Participation Function / 25
2.5 Accounting for the Changes in Female Labor Force Participation in Urban China / 35
2.6 Conclusion / 44
2.7 Appendix / 46

Chapter 3 Social Norms and Female Labor Force Participation in China 52

3.1 Introduction / 52
3.2 Social and Gender Identity Norms in China / 57
3.3 Literature Review / 59
3.4 Empirical Analysis / 62
3.5 Estimation Results / 67

3.6 Robustness Checks / 79

3.7 Conclusion / 87

Chapter 4 Impact of Rural-to-Urban Migration on Labor Market Conditions of Urban Residents in China ······ 89

4.1 Introduction / 89

4.2 Historical Background / 92

4.3 Literature Review / 94

4.4 Empirical Analysis / 97

4.5 Estimation Results / 105

4.6 Conclusion / 111

Bibliography / 113

Acknowledgments / 122

Chapter 1
Introduction

This book seeks to understand the mysterious declining labor force participation rate of the wage workers with urban registration in China since the 1990s. Both male and female labor market attachment has dramatically declined in China during the last three decades as the country makes an transition from a centrally-planned economy to a market-oriented economy. Before the late 1980s, the government typically assigned a lifetime job to each new entrant to the labor market who was able-bodied, so both male and female labor force participation rates in urban China were almost universal at that time; whereas in more recent years people are increasingly more likely to exit the formal labor market and their participation rate has dropped to around 75% (Feng, Hu and Moffitt, 2015). The decline in labor market participation is especially drastic for the female group. This labor market trend in China reverses the pattern of increasing female labor force participation experienced in the U. S. and other major developed economies in the past several decades.

There is sizable body of empirical work studying the evolution and determination of the labor participation rate in developed countries. The explanations for the rising female labor force participation in the U. S. include the increase in women's real wage and education (Eckstein and Lifshitz, 2011), the technological advances in consumer durables (Greenwood, Seshadri and Yorukoglu, 2004) and the expansion of the service sector (Goldin, 1990). Similar socioeconomic changes have also taken place in China since the 1990s, yet there has been a continuous decline in women's involvement in the formal labor market. The discrepancy between theoretical prediction and observed labor market trends is one of the major motivations of our study. In particular, we intend to understand the evolution and determination of labor supply in China during a period of rapid socioeconomic transformation. The period from the late 1980s to the early 2010s is the main focus of the empirical analysis in this book.

Recent studies explain the puzzling decline of female labor supply in China have focused on factors such as the changing family structure (Maurer-Fazio et al., 2009; Shen, Zhang and Yan, 2012), the changing child care system after the economic reform (Du and Dong, 2010), and the rising housing price (Fu, Liao, and Zhang, 2016). Our research makes three important contributions to the existing literature. Firstly, regarding the evolution of labor supply in China, we use decomposition technique to systematically relate the decrease in female labor force participation to the socio-economic changes happening in China during the same period, and assess the respective contributions of all the relevant factors. Most of the existing studies only concentrate on assessing the contribution of a specific factor, and most of the efforts have been made in assessing the contributions of supply-side factors. In order to fill in this gap, we include both demand-side and supply-side factors in our empirical specifications and comprehensively assess the contribution of each factor by adopting both linear and non-linear decomposition technique.

Secondly, in regards to the determination of labor supply in China, we suggest two new and complementary angles which have not been explored in the existing literature: social norm and rural-to-urban migration. Particularly, in Chapter 3, we investigate the impact of social norms on married women's labor supply decisions in China, and find a strong and robust positive correlation between the labor supply behavior of a married woman and the former work experience of her mother-in-law. To our knowledge, we are among the first to examine the impact of social norms on female labor supply in a fast-growing transition economy, which has witnessed drastic socioeconomic changes since the 1980s, and also the first to provide empirical evidence to both of the mechanisms underlying this observed intergeneration correlation. In Chapter 4, we examine the impact of rural-to-urban migration on the labor market conditions of urban residents in China. Our estimation results indicate the inflow of rural migrants reduces the wage and labor supply of competing urban residents. We contribute to the existing literature by adopting the skill cells approach at the local level to study the impact of rural migrant flow on local economies. Also, we implement the instrumental variable strategy and use two sets of instrumental variables unexplored in the previous studies on rural migrants. The significant findings gained from these two angles are consistent with the labor market trends observed in China since the 1990s, and therefore, can be potentially used to account for the mysterious declining labor force participation rate in urban China.

Last but not least, our research contributes to the empirical literature on the movement and determination of labor supply behavior in developing countries which is relatively scarce compared to the studies on developed countries. To examine the evolution and determination of labor supply in the context of a developing country is important because developing countries and developed countries are very different in terms of cultural background and institutional setting. Additionally, as a result of the economic reform, China provides great experimental fields to answer many general economic inquiries and we would like to fully utilize this opportunity. For instance, in chapter 3, we chose China as a specimen to investigate the impact of social norms on married women's labor force participation decisions because China has witnessed significant changes in gender norms during the past 30 years as a consequence of the state-sector restructuring; in chapter 4, we use rural-to-urban migration to provide new evidence and contribute to the old theoretical debate on the relationship between migration inflow and the labor market conditions of local residents because China's rural-to-urban migration is the largest migration movements in human history and China's *Hukou* system provides additional support to the closed labor market assumption required for the main empirical strategy used in this chapter.

This book consists of three major parts. Chapter 2 investigates the evolution of female labor supply in urban China, chapter 3 and chapter 4 study different determinants of labor supply in China. In particular, chapter 2 decomposes the decline of female labor force participation into different sources; chapter 3 studies how does the former employment status of a woman's mother-in-law affect her current labor market participation decision; and chapter 4 explores how does the inflow of rural migrants affect the labor supply decisions of urban residents.

In chapter 2, we use a time series of cross-sections from the Chinese Household Income Project Series (CHIPS) to systematically relate the decrease in female labor force participation to the socio-economic changes happening in China during the same period, and assess their respective contributions. We include both demand-side and supply-side factors in our empirical specifications and adopt both linear and non-linear decomposition technique to conduct the analysis. The estimation results show that during 1988 – 1995, changes in population age distribution and family size both contribute, during 1995 – 2002, age effect dominates, and during 2002 – 2007, non-labor income effect dominates in explaining the decreasing trend in female labor force participation.

In chapter 3, we investigate the impact of social norms on married women's labor supply decisions in China. Using data from the China General Social Survey (CGSS) and the China Family Panel Studies (CFPS), we find a strong and robust positive correlation between the labor supply behavior of a married woman and the former work experience of her mother-in-law. We also provide empirical evidence for the underlying channels through which mothers-in-law's working status may affect the labor force participation decisions of the wives. Our estimation results indicate that being raised by a working mother influences both a man's attitude toward gender roles and his household productivity, and therefore married women whose mothers-in-law were not working are themselves significantly less likely to participate in the labor force.

In the last chapter, we examine the impact of rural-to-urban migration on the labor market conditions of urban residents. Specifically, we use the data of the 2000 and the 2005 Census and the skill cells approach at the local level to estimate the possible employment and earnings displacement effects of rural-to-urban migration on urban residents. Multiple sets of instrumental variable have been used to address the potential endogeneity problems associated with the rural migrant ratio in a city. The estimation results are consistent with the predictions of the textbook model of a competitive labor market, indicating the inflow of rural migrants reduces the wage and labor supply of competing urban residents.

Chapter 2
The Evolution of Female Labor Force Participation in Urban China

Female labor force participation rate in China has been declining rapidly since the 1990s. Using a time series of cross-sections from the Chinese Household Income Project Series (CHIPS), this chapter attempts to systematically relate the decrease in female labor force participation to the socio-economic changes happening in China during the same period, and assess their respective contributions. Adopting the linear and non-linear decomposition techniques, the results show that during 1988 – 1995, changes in population age distribution and family size both contribute, during 1995 – 2002, age effect dominates, and during 2002 – 2007, non-labor income effect dominates in explaining the decreasing trend in female labor force participation.

2.1 Introduction

Starting from the late 1980s, despite the rapid economic growth, China's labor force participation rate (LFPR) has begun to decline at the aggregate level as well as for each demographic group, which suggests that an increasing share of the working population are inclined not to search for jobs. More drastic decline is found for the female group. Meanwhile, China's population age structure has experienced tremendous changes as a consequence of the One Child Policy implemented in 1979. The size of the working age population has begun to show signs of decreasing in 2012. A shrinking working age population with a decreasing LFPR casts shadows on the pension system and the sustained economic growth of contemporary China.

Besides the policy concerns, the declining labor force participation rate also poses an interesting empirical question. The traditional static neoclassic labor supply theory emphasizes the role played by the changes in wage rate as the key determinant in the movement of labor force participation rate, and predicts unambiguously positive wage effect on labor participation. Based on it, the rapid rise in real wage level has been used to successfully explain the increasing trend in female labor force participation in the United States and many other developed countries over the past century. However, we have not observed this positive correlation between wage rate and labor participation in China. According to the calculations of the author using the data from Chinese Household Income Project Series (CHIPS), with female real wage level increasing more than 4 times from 1988 to 2007, female labor force participation rate has decreased from 0.93 to 0.69 during the same period. Since the positive wage participation elasticity is also found in my estimation using the cross-sectional data, it must be the case that the wage effect has been dominated by the effects of other social-economic changes which would contribute positively to this declining trend in female labor force participation.

There is a sizable body of empirical work studying the evolution in labor participation rate in developed countries. In these studies, a variety of potential explanations have been proposed. Those explanations cover both demand-side and supply-side factors, where the demand-side factors emphasize the movements in the market wage rate as discussed in Juhn (1992) and the supply-side factors highlight the shifts in the reservation wage (Parsons, 1980). In addition, there are also studies trying to incorporate and assess the contributions of both supply-side and demand-side factors to the changing labor force participation using decomposition technique (Gomulka and Stern, 1990).

However, the empirical work on the movement of labor force participation in developing countries is relatively scarce. Additionally, most existing studies only assess the contribution of a specific factor. For instance, the contribution of changing family structure has been examined in Shen et al. (2012) and Maurer-Fazio et al. (2011). They use different datasets and reach the same conclusion that co-residing with parents promotes labor force participation of urban prime-age women because parents can assist with household work. This finding could help explain the downward trend in female labor force participation since there is a decreasing tendency of intergenerational co-residence in nowadays China. More often than not, literature on this respect focuses on assessing the contributions of supply-side factors, whereas demand-side factors are always neglected in their models and the wage effect on labor force participation has not been properly evaluated.

In order to fill in this gap and to systematically relate the decrease in female labor force participation to the socio-economic changes happening in China during the same period and comprehensively assess their relative contributions, in this chapter, I use decomposition technique and include both demand-side and supply-side factors in my model. Specifically, I first estimate the separate participation equations for each sample year, and then decompose the changes in labor force participation rate into the portion which can be explained by the change in measured population characteristics, i. e. the demand-side and supply-side factors included in my empirical specification, and the portion which can be explained by the rest, i. e. the changes in labor participation behavior. Following most work adopting this technique, the contributions of the difference in endowments, i. e. quantity effect, are being concentrated on in this chapter. The main findings indicate during 1988 – 1995, changes in population age distribution and family size both contribute to the decline in female labor force participation rate, and respectively account for 22.1% and 16.6% of the total decline; during 1995 – 2002, age effect dominates and contributes to 73.4% of the total decline, while the increase in non-labor income accounts for 17.8% of the total decline; and during 2002 – 2007, non-labor income effect dominates and accounts for 48.9% of the total decline.

The rest of this chapter is organized as follows. Section 2.2 reviews the literature on the evolution and determination of female labor supply; Section 2.3 describes the data and documents the stylized facts; Section 2.4 estimates the participation function for each sample year; Section 2.5 decomposes the total decline in female labor force participation rate; and Section 2.6 concludes.

2.2 Literature Review

There is abundant literature on the evolution and determination of labor supply, most of which focuses on the labor supply behavior at the intensive margin. Blundell and MaCurdy (1999) provides a comprehensive review on the alternative approaches to labor supply modeling. Another extensive survey of labor supply models is given by Blundell, MaCurdy, and Meghir (2007), focusing on the issues that arise from unobserved heterogeneity, non-participation and dynamics. Particularly, Killingsworth and Heckman (1986) surveys the theoretical and empirical literature on female labor supply.

Theoretically, neoclassical labor supply models treat individual labor supply decision as a consumer choice problem regarding the trade-off between consumption and leisure. The extensions of the basic model include the incorporation of household production and intra-familial decisions, and the life-cycle model. For married women, the labor supply behavior is always analyzed in the household context, as in the standard unitary and collective models of family labor supply. In more recent years, dynamic structural female labor supply modeling has becoming increasingly prevalent, yet this approach is very computationally intensive. [1] Empirically, wage and non-labor income, household structure, educa-

---

[1] For instance, see Eckstein, Z., and Lifshitz, O. Dynamic female labor supply. Econometrica, 2011, 79 (6): 1675–1726.

tion, fertility, household production technology, and culture are common factors being proposed to explain female labor supply decision. Most of the empirical studies utilize the data from developed countries.

In regards to the wage effect on labor force participation, Juhn (1992) uses the micro data from the Current Population Surveys to analyze the decline in labor force participation among prime age men in the United States during 1967 – 1987 from the perspective of changing wage structure. She finds the decline in labor market participation is particularly pronounced among less-educated men and men with lower earning potential, and it happens concurrently with the decreasing real wage for the same group of men. After estimating the participation functions and conducting decomposition analysis, she concludes that the change in wage structure (demand-side factors) could account for most of the decrease in male LFPR from the early 1970s through the late 1980s, while the change in supply-side factors dominates in explaining the initial decline from the late 1960s to the early 1970s.

For the female group, Mincer (1962) first separates male and female wages and investigates their impacts on female labor force participation separately. He interprets the impact of husbands' wage on female labor force participation rate as income effect, and married women's own wage effect as substitution effect. Labor supply of married women is positively affected by their own wages and negatively affected by the wages of their husbands. However, this perspective has shown decreasing power in explaining the change in female labor supply over the years, because the research on developed countries generally suggests a declining trend in both own wage elasticity and cross wage elasticity among married women (Blau and Kahn, 2005). This trend could be attributed to the increasing divorce rate as well as the changing perception from viewing jobs as means to earn an income to careers among married women. Nevertheless, whether this conclusion could be extended to developing countries remains to be examined.

The influence of non-labor income on labor supply behavior has also been investigated in many existing literature. For the male group, non-participation benefit has been explored as one form of non-labor income, while husbands' earnings are always explored as non-labor income for married women. For instance, Parsons (1980) tests the hypothesis that the rapid expansion of welfare alternatives to work leads to the decline in male labor force participation rate. The results obtained from cross-sectional estimation and time-series projection are consistent with his hypothesis. Data used in this chapter is the older men's (45 – 59 years old) sample of the National Longitudinal Surveys (NLS), and this angle might be helpful in explaining the labor force participation behavior of the elder group.

Female labor supply behavior has also been studied in the context of her family structure. For instance, due to the cultural tradition of family-based elder care in Asia, the co-residency status with parents and in-laws is always being considered in the studies on the female labor supply behavior in Asian countries. However, the empirical work in this field has not reached any consensus on the net effects of co-residence. On one hand, taking care of elderly parents needs time and may reduce the labor supply of married women; yet on the other hand, elderly parents could assist with housework and childcare and thereby encourages the labor supply of the female members in a family. Positive effects of co-residence on female labor supply are more often reported in the empirical literature. For instance, Ogawa and Ermisch (1996) use the 1990 Japanese national survey data and their results suggest younger married women living in the multi-generational households are more likely to take paid employment, indicating the importance of the child-care role played by the women's parents or parents-in-law.

There is also vast empirical literature on the role of fertility in labor force participation decisions of married women. The relationship between fertility and female labor supply is well established in theory but complicated to identify due to the endogeneity of fertility. To overcome this issue, exogenous variations in family size are often used as instrumental variable (IV). The most widely used instrument is twins. Besides the twins IV, Angrist and Evans (1996) suggest an instrument of sibling-sex composition. Another instrument is developed by Agüero and Marks (2008). They propose to use an indicator variable reflecting women's infertility status at child-bearing age as an instrument for childbearing. Compared with the results gained using Ordinary Least Squares (OLS), the IV approach generally indicates smaller or no effects of childbearing on female labor supply.

Marriage market conditions can also affect female labor supply by influencing women's bargaining power in the marriage (Becker, 2009; Grossbard-Shechtman, 1984; Chiappori et al., 2002). These conditions could be investigated independently using exogenous shock or incorporated in the framework of collective labor supply as distribution factors (Chiappori et al., 2002). Literature from this angle mainly focuses on two types of marriage market conditions: sex ratio (Angrist, 2002; Amuedo-Dorantes and Grossbard, 2007) and divorce law (Bargain et al., 2012). For instance, Angrist (2002) finds a higher sex ratio can exert a large negative effect on female labor force participation rate; Amuedo-Dorantes and Grossbard (2007) also reach the same conclusion and their results further suggest the sex ratio effect might be stronger among less educated women.

The evolution and determination of female labor supply has also been studied from the perspective of cultural impact (Fernández, Fogli and Olivetti, 2004; Farré and Vella, 2007; Fortin, 2009; Fernández, 2013). For instance, Fernández (2013) points out that cultural and female labor participation could be co-determined and develops a model of married women's work decisions to explain the evolution of female labor force participation over the century.

Compared to the sizable literature using the U.S. data, empirical studies on China's female labor supply are relatively scarce, and most of them use cross-section data and approach this issue from a single angle. For instance, Li and Zax (2003) investigate the labor supply behavior in urban China at the intensive margin using the CHIPS 1995 dataset. In this paper, individual labor supply behavior is studied under the framework of the unitary model of family labor supply, and the two-stage least squares technique is adopted to address the endogeneity problem associated with one's own wage and family income. The results indicate positive compensated wage effect and negative income effect present in China's urban worker. These effects are statistically significant in most specifications and are larger in magnitude for non-household heads and women.

There is also literature trying to explain the decreasing trend in female labor force participation rate in China since the late 1980s. Among the studies investigating female labor supply behavior at the extensive margin, most of them did not include demand-side factors in their model, but mainly focus on assessing the influence of a specific supply-side factor which correlates to the shift in women's reservation wage.① Yao and Tan (2005) investigate the impact of husband's income on female labor force participation and find the increase in husband's income can only account for 12.87% of the decrease in female LFPR during 1995 – 2002, and this impact is declining over the years. They conclude that the deteriorating market opportunity is the main reason causing this decline, but did not provide rigorous analysis to support this argument.

Effects of the changing family structure and child-care pattern on women's labor force participation decisions have also been investigated empirically in order to explain the downward trend in female labor force participation. Shen et al. (2012) use the data of middle-aged women in Chinese eastern provinces and find co-residing with parents promotes women's labor force participation because parents could provide assistance to household work. Maurer-Fazio et al. (2011) also reach the same conclusion using census data of 1982, 1990 and 2000. This finding can help explain the downward trend in female labor force participation since there is a decreasing tendency of intergenerational co-residence in nowadays China.

A public funded childcare system had been established in China under centrally planned economy. However, this system has been eroded substantially since the economic reform.② Du and Dong (2010) find that following the child care reform, women's labor force participation has been increasingly dependent on the access to informal caregivers. Their findings also suggest the tension be-

---

① For a detailed description of the classification on demand-side and supply-side factors, please refer to Juhn (1992) and Juhn and Potter (2006).

② Du and Dong (2010) provide a thorough overview of China's childcare system reform.

tween income earning and child-rearing has been strengthened by the childcare reform, especially for the socioeconomically disadvantaged women who have no access to informal childcare and cannot afford formal childcare. Kilburn and Datar (2002) investigate the role of childcare centers and their impact on female labor force participation using difference in differences (DID) strategy. Their results suggest that the presence of childcare centers can exert positive effects on female labor force participation decision.

Based on the literature review, this paper contributes to the existing studies by investigating female labor participation using data from developing countries under a standard static labor supply framework. Among the research using China's data, to my knowledge, this paper is among the first to use a time-series of cross-sectional data and the decomposition technique to study the decreasing female labor force participation rate in China since the 1990s. In addition, instead of only focusing on the impact of a specific factor, this paper assesses and summarizes the contributions of the changing distribution in all the relevant factors involved in the static labor supply model. Last but not least, the effects of demand-side factors have also been considered in my study, so have several econometric issues which have always been neglected in China's studies, such as the correction of selective bias, and the treatment of the potential endogeneity problem associated with non-labor income.

2.3 Data and Descriptive Patterns

2.3.1 Data Description

In this paper, I use the data from the Chinese Household Income Project Series (CHIPS), which is a joint effort of Chinese and foreign researchers and conducted by the National Bureau of Statistics (NBS). CHIPS is a repeated cross-sectional dataset and is collected for urban and rural households of China in 1988, 1995, 2002 and 2007. Starting from 2002, a survey of rural-to-urban migrants was added to reflect the growing importance of rural-to-urban migration since the mid – 1990s. Thus, CHIPS 2002 and 2007 are composed of three parts: the urban household survey, the rural household survey, and the rural-to-urban migrant household survey. The purpose of CHIPS is to track the dynamics of the income distribution in China, yet its rich labor market information also generates research of a wide range of topics.

The CHIPS data was collected from different regions of China and is nationally representative. The number of provinces covered in four waves of the survey are 10, 11, 12 and 16 respectively. ①For the urban household survey, there are 9 009 households and 3 1827 individuals in 1988, 6 931 households and 21 694 individuals in 1995, and 6 835 households and 20 632 individuals in 2002. For CHIPS 2007, the publicly available sample is the additional sample of 5 000 urban households with 14 551 individuals in nine provinces. To make the rotation comparable over the sample years, I keep the 5 provinces which are present in all four waves of the publicly available survey, including: Jiangsu, Anhui, Henan, Hubei and Guangdong.

Since my study focuses on the labor supply behavior of female urban workers (employees), I use the CHIPS datasets of urban individual and urban household in my analysis. Individuals who are employers or self-employed are excluded, and the sample is restricted to females aged 16 – 55 and males aged 16 – 60. Also, I only include individuals with urban registration (*Hukou*). ② I elimi-

---

①② Household Registration System (*Hukou* system) imposes strict restrictions on rural-to-urban migration. Up until the late 1980s, those restrictions were gradually loosened due to the increasing demand for rural labor in urban areas. I restrict the analysis to urban workers with *Hukou* since abundant literature (e. g. Dmurger et al., 2009) shows that rural migrant workers and urban workers exhibit very different patterns in their labor market behavior. For instance, the labor force participation rate of rural migrant married women in urban China is lower than their non-migrant counterpart since many of them migrate to cities to support their husbands and children (Maurer-Fazio et al., 2009). However, it should be noted that Household registration type is only asked in the surveys of 2002 and 2007.

nate full-time students in most part of my analysis. ① For the estimation of the static labor supply model and the decomposition analysis, besides the above sample restrictions, I limit the subsample to be married women whose husbands are also non-migrant, neither employers nor self-employed, and aged 16 – 60. I choose the sample to be married women in my empirical analysis since married women constitute 86.77% of the remaining sample after I impose all the other restrictions. ② Another reason for using the subsample of married women in the empirical analysis is that it would greatly increase the variation in the non-labor income variable. After imposing all the sample restrictions, the sample sizes are 3 694, 2 198, 2 060, and 1 004 for the years of 1988, 1995, 2002, and 2007 respectively.

The labor force participation rate is generally defined as the proportion of the individuals who are either employed or unemployed among the working age population. ③ In this chapter, a participation indicator is constructed for every individual in the sample to calculate the aggregate labor force participation rate. Non-participation is defined as those who are disabled, or retired, or currently students, or waiting for job assignments or entering higher schools, or homemakers doing housework, or in other situations. If none of these cases are true, the person is defined as a participant and a participation indicator is generated. The participation indicator is a dummy variable equals one if participates and zero otherwise.

The wage variable refers to the annual wage income and is constructed as the sum of wages, bonuses and subsidies, allowances, and other labor income from the work unit. Information on second jobs is also included if the relevant questions were asked. Income-in-kind is excluded due to the lack of individual information

---

① Except for the statistics reported in Panel A of Table 2.1 and Figure 2.2, all the descriptive patterns in Section 2.3 and all the empirical analysis in Section 2.4 are calculated and estimated by excluding full-time students.

② The proportion of married women is based on the calculation for years 1995 – 2007, since marital status was not asked in the survey of 1988. Additionally, this high marriage rate can also be confirmed by other data sources. For instance, according to the calculation of Maurer-Fazio et al. based on the 2000 census data, the proportions of single women among the women aged 30 – 34 and the women aged 25 – 39 are only 1.3%, and 0.5% respectively (Maurer-Fazio et al., 2009).

③ Unemployed is defined for the people who are not working but actively searching for work.

in the 1988 survey. If only the monthly wage is reported, as in 1988 and 2007, I multiplies monthly wage by 12 months since most Chinese workers work full-time. The detailed construction methods of the participation indicator and wage variable are discussed in Appendix A.

For married women, non-labor income generally consists of property income, transfer income, and husband's income. In the regression, non-labor income is constructed at household level, since individual information on non-labor income is unavailable for the years 1988 and 2007. [1]Specifically, non-labor income is calculated as the sum of interest, dividend, rent of the household, and husband's wage income (Heim, 2007). Transfer income has been excluded from the construction due to its obvious endogenous concern to the labor force participation decision, which is also the standard method employed by labor economists (e.g. Moffitt, 2012). Husband's income is also potentially endogenous as suggested by theory of collective household labor supply; however, I include it in the construction of the non-labor income variable to perform preliminary estimation of a simple framework, and to increase the variation in the non-labor income variable because most individuals do not have property income reported and most of the values are zero among those who have reported them.

Education attainment is grouped into three categories: middle school and below, high school and tech, and university and above. Potential experience is constructed using *age-years of schooling* – 6. [2]Household head indicator is also generated to account for potential family responsibility. To control for family structure, two indicators are con-structed in order to capture the co-residency status with elderly parents (>60 years old) or younger children (<15 years old). Nine cohort groups are defined at 5 – year intervals. The provincial dummies are also constructed to account for the regional differences and cultural effects. All the nominal variables are adjusted in real terms using a set of urban provincial-level spatial price

---

[1] In the empirical analysis, I control for the number of household members in a family.

[2] Data on "years of schooling" is not available for the year of 1988 and has to be imputed for that year following Li (2003).

deflators developed by Brandt and Holz (2006) instead of the commonly used urban provincial consumer price index. ① I adopt this method because, compared with the traditional method, it accounts for the difference of local living cost across different provinces, and thus is more reasonable for spatial comparison.

2.3.2 Labor Force Participation in Urban China (1988 – 2007)

Over the past 30 years, China's economy has transitioned from a central planned regime to a much more market-oriented one. Along with the rapid economic growth, the labor market in China has undergone tremendous transformation as well. Before the late 1980s, the government typically assigned a lifetime job to each new entrant to the labor market who was able-bodied, so both male and female labor force participation rates in urban China were very high at that time. This abnormally high LFPR has begun to decline at the aggregate level since the 1990s. In order to identify the micro-pattern of this change, i. e. which group of people are declining and to what extent, I disaggregate the overall sample into subgroups and calculate the labor force participation rate for each subgroup.

From Table 2.1, we observe that during 1988 – 2007, the labor force participation rate is declining for both genders, and the female group is decreasing much more rapidly compared to their male counterpart. In addition, male LFPR is relatively stable after the initial decrease during 1988 – 1995. This pattern looks very different from the pattern observed in the U. S. data documented in many studies②: a long-term trend of increasing female labor force participation along with declining male labor force participation since 1950. ③

---

① Brandt and Holz's updated version of "provincial-level basket values (price levels) for 1984 – 2010" could be found online.

② It is also different from the labor market trends observed in other developed economies (Cahuc, 2004).

③ There is a reversal trend in female labor force participation rate since 2000 observed in the U. S. data.

Chapter 2
The Evolution of Female Labor Force Participation in Urban China

Since the decline in total labor force participation rate in China is mainly due to the rapid decrease in female labor participation since the late 1980s, the rest of this book will focus on the labor force participation behavior of the female sample. To see the pattern clearly, I disaggregate the female sample by age, education level, marital status, and cohort group. Then I compare the labor force participation rate among different subgroups. The results reveal very marked patterns.

Table 2.1 Labor Force Participation Rate in Urban China (1988 – 2007)

	1988	1995	2002	2007	Change (1988 – 2007)
Overall	0.950	0.829	0.792	0.756	-0.194
Male	0.965	0.858	0.845	0.822	-0.143
Female	0.934	0.800	0.737	0.688	-0.246
Women					
Panel A. Age					
16 – 19	0.959	0.209	0.057	0.035	-0.924
20 – 24	0.994	0.908	0.577	0.585	-0.409
25 – 29	0.998	0.958	0.912	0.854	-0.144
30 – 34	0.998	0.986	0.990	0.904	-0.094
35 – 39	0.994	0.978	0.937	0.891	-0.103
40 – 44	0.991	0.968	0.964	0.874	-0.117
45 – 49	0.926	0.787	0.851	0.771	-0.155
50 – 55	0.546	0.376	0.319	0.282	-0.264
Panel B. Education					
Middle school and below	0.890	0.785	0.638	0.576	-0.314
High school and tech	0.983	0.943	0.912	0.787	-0.196
University and above	0.993	0.963	0.945	0.933	-0.060
Panel C. Marital Status					
Married		0.866	0.814	0.752	-0.114
Never married		0.970	0.949	0.837	-0.133
Divorce/Wid.		0.651	0.729	0.604	-0.047

Source: Author's Calculations using Chinese Household Income Project Series.

Panel A of Table 2.1 compares female labor force participation by age group.① We can see that certain age groups show lower labor force participation rates and experience faster decrease than other groups over the survey years. Specifically, younger groups show significant drops during sample years: from 0.959 in 1988 to 0.035 in 2007 for the age group 16 – 19 (– 92 percentage points), and 0.994 to 0.585 for the age group 20 – 24 (– 41 percentage points). This phenomenon might be caused by rising school attendance rates. Especially for the age group 20 – 24, the 1999 college enrollment expansion may serve a potential explanation for the significant decrease. The prime working age groups (25 – 44) show moderate decrease by 11 percentage points on average during the sample years. The elder groups 40 – 55 show faster drop than the prime working age groups as well, especially for the age group 50 – 55. In the urban areas of China, the mandatory retirement age is 55 for female cadres, and 50 for female workers. The changing retirement behavior may cause the large drop in the LFPR of the elder groups. Also, I suspect there might be other reasons contributing to this phenomenon, such as the cohort effect for certain age cohorts (e.g. sent-down cohort).

Panel B of Table 2.1 documents female LFPR by education level. Female LFPR is dropping over the survey years for women at each education level, but is lower and decreasing faster for the less educated group. Particularly, the decrease in labor force participation rate from 1988 to 2007 for "Middle School and Below", "High School and Tech", and "University and Above" are 31 percentage points, 20 percentage points and 6 percentage points respectively. It also should be noted that while the LFPR of "Middle School and Below" group declines steadily over time, the gap between groups of "High School and Tech" and "University and Above" does not distinctively widen up until 2002. Moreover, since the "High School and Tech" group constitutes the highest proportion in the population among the three subgroups (except for the year of 1988), the

---

① Full-time students are included in the calculation of the statistics in Panel A.

Chapter 2
The Evolution of Female Labor Force Participation in Urban China

participation behavior of this group should be very much worthy to notice.

Figure 2.1 portrays female LFPR by age and education.① Over the sample years, the participation gap among people with different education attainments has widened up at each age level. From Figure 2.1, we observe that the greatest drop in participation rate is experienced by the people of lower education levels and people from younger age groups, especially during the more recent years. This seems similar to the pattern detected for the declining employment-population ratio in the U.S. during 1999 – 2007 (Moffitt, 2012).

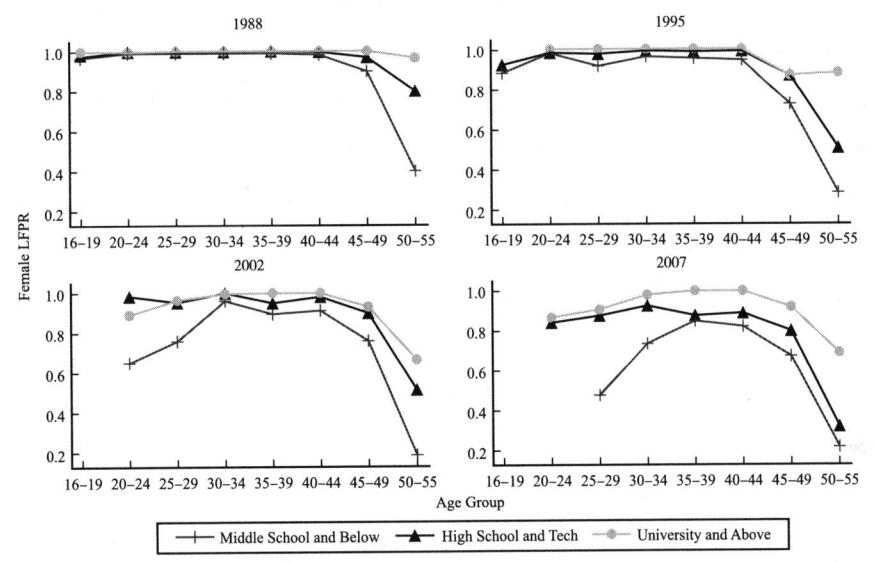

Figure 2.1 Female LFPR in Urban China by Education and Age (1988 – 2007)

Source: Author's calculations using Chinese Household Income Project Series.

There might be various reasons attributed to this phenomenon. One of them could be the impact of the remarkable increase in migrant workers in cities, which is the result of loosen restrictions for rural-urban migration in China since the late 1980s. Most of the rural migrant workers are young and less-educated, and concentrated in the lower-skilled sector; thus it could constitute supply

---

① The corresponding Table 2.5 could be found in Appendix B in this chapter. I delete some groups with less than 10 observations, which is the reason for the missing points in Table 2.5 and Figure 2.1.

shocks to the urban workers in similar situations. Another potential explanation is the changing pattern of child-rearing behavior of the lowest education group. It is described from Figure 2.1 that the participation rate of this group has been decreasing significantly before age 30 over the sample years, which may indicate greater impact of child-rearing behavior for the less-educated women.

Another interesting finding from Figure 2.1 is that the turning point of labor force participation behavior is around age 40 for people of each education group. It corresponds to the "4050 phenomenon" which refers to the difficulty in reemployment for a specific age group (40 for female and 50 for male) if being laid off. This observation implies that the dismal market opportunities for women older than 40 may play a role in explaining the decline in labor supply of this age group.

Additionally, it is well established theoretically and empirically that female labor force participation is influenced by marital status, and it is also shown in panel C of Table 2.1. Labor force participation rate for both single and married women are declining over 1995 and 2007,① while the decline in the labor supply of single women is slightly larger. The divorce and widowed group is very small in sample size, but since it shows different pattern from both married and never married group, I did not combine it with the other two groups and list it here for reference.

Panel C of Table 2.1 shows that never married women have higher LFPR than married women for all sample years, which is consistent with the pattern observed in the U. S.. However, for trend comparison, China and the U. S. exhibit opposite patterns. In China, female LFPR is declining at both aggregate level and for women of different marital status; while in the U. S. , it shows substantial increase at the aggregate level since 1962, which was primarily driven by the increased participation rate of married women, with almost constant single female LFPR (Eckstein and Lifshitz, 2011). However, it is important to bear in mind that the marriage rate is very high in China among prime-age women and the sin-

---

① Marital status was not asked in the survey of 1988.

Chapter 2
The Evolution of Female Labor Force Participation in Urban China

gle group is relatively small in sample size compared to the situation in the U. S. . Thus, the empirical analysis in this paper mainly focuses on the labor participation behavior of married women.

I also compare the female labor force participation rate across generations. In contrast to the pattern found in the U. S. in Juhn and Potter (2006), Figure 2.2 shows that in China women are less willing to participate in the labor market compared to their earlier birth cohorts at the same age. ① Specifically, cohort 1955 and cohort 1960 behave similarly, cohort 1965 began to diverge with their earlier cohorts, and the curves of the later cohorts tend to decline. Another interesting pattern shown in this figure is that beginning with cohort 1970, the female LFPR becomes significantly lower during the ages of child-bearing (aged 25 – 30), which may indicate changing child-rearing behavior and require further investigation. ②

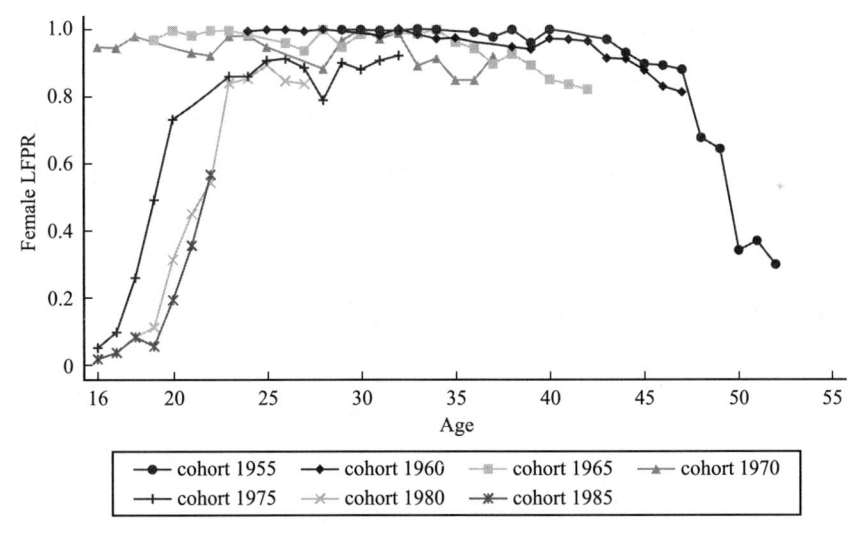

Figure 2.2　Female LFPR in Urban China by Cohort (1988 – 2007)

Source: Author's calculations using Chinese Household Income Project Series.

---

① Full-time students are included in the calculation of the statistics in Figure 2.2.

② Another event which might be relevant is that Labor Law requires employer to sign the contract with their employees since the year 1995.

In sum, the figures and tables above reveal that female labor force participation rate in urban China has been declining during 1988 – 2007 at both aggregate level and for every subgroup by age, education, marital status and cohort, yet the extents of the decline are uneven for different subgroups. We observe more severe decline in female labor market participation for the younger and older age groups, the less-educated group, the single women group, and the more recent cohorts.

The sample statistics of the married women are presented in Table 2.2. The statistics show that during 1988 – 2007, women's education level, real wage income, age, and non-labor in-come have all exhibited upwards trends, while household size and the proportion of women co-residing with children under age 15 have shown shrinking decrease. For instance, in 1988, there are 69% of urban non-migrant married women in working age living with their children aged 15 or under, while in 2007, this proportion has dropped to 42%. The increase in education level, real wage, and the decrease in the proportion of young children's presence are expected to increase women's propensity to participate in the labor force. The increase in non-labor income might work in the opposite direction.

Table 2.2   Descriptive Statistics: CHIPS Data (1988 – 2007)

	1988		1995		2002		2007	
	Mean	S.D.	Mean	S.D.	Mean	S.D.	Mean	S.D.
Real wage (¥)	1 625.02	605.31	2 227.00	1 257.26	3 342.89	2 400.49	6 026.74	3 860.85
Non-labor income (¥)	2 031.92	791.19	2 900.54	1 554.82	4 537.97	2 823.42	9 501.41	8 197.67
Age	38.75	7.64	39.79	7.26	41.50	7.38	39.93	8.40
Co-reside with children (< 15)	0.69	0.46	0.56	0.50	0.44	0.50	0.42	0.49
Number of household member	3.66	0.93	3.28	0.72	3.18	0.73	3.15	0.79

continued

	1988		1995		2002		2007	
	Mean	S. D.	Mean	S. D.	Mean	S. D.	Mean	S. D.
Education attainment (%)								
Middle school and below	59.50		45.50		32.09		25.70	
High school and tech	37.85		51.14		62.86		63.05	
University and above	2.65		3.37		5.05		11.25	
Observations	3 694.00		2 198.00		2 060.00		1 004.00	

Source: Author's Calculations using Chinese Household Income Project Series.

2.4 Estimation of the Participation Function

From Section 2.3, we found that female labor force participation has been decreasing at the aggregate level and within each demographic group. To see how labor force participation is determined, participation function has to be estimated for each sample year and labor supply decisions need to be investigated at the extensive margin. Most studies on labor supply focus on decisions at the intensive margin. Although many explanatory variables involved in the labor supply decisions at the extensive and intensive margin are the same, the theory predictions of these explanatory variables on the participation decision and the hours of work decision could be different in both sign and magnitude, since these two problems are essentially different. For the labor supply decisions at the intensive margin, marginal utilities are involved; while for the labor supply decisions at the extensive margin, comparison of utility levels is required.

2.4.1 Static Labor Supply Theory

Static labor supply model has been widely used to estimate the decisions of work hours as well as the decisions of participation or employment, while for women, the latter one has been regarded to be particularly important. Static labor supply theory models individual's decisions of whether to work, and how many hours to work as functions of his or her market wage and non-labor income.

To illustrate the simple static labor supply theory, suppose an individual's utility function is $U(C, L \mid Z, e)$, where C is the composite consumer good consumed by this individual, and L is the leisure time for him or her. Z represents the observable individual characteristics and e represents the unobservable individual factors. Individual i maximizes his or her utility subject to the budget constraint $PC \leq R + W \times H$, where P is the unit price of the composite good, R is the non-labor income per period, W is the wage rate for individual i and H is the working hours. The time constraint is $H + L = T$, where T is the total available time per period.

Applying Kuhn-Tucker conditions to solve this utility maximization problem for individual i, then for an working individual, interior optimum is achieved and working hours is determined by the equilibrium condition $\frac{W}{P} = M(W \times H + R, T - H)$, where M is the marginal rate of substitution between consumption and leisure; while non-participation happens if the corner solution is achieved for this optimization problem, i. e.

$$U_L - \mu W > 0 \quad \Rightarrow \quad W < \frac{U_L}{\mu} \quad \Rightarrow \quad L^* = T \quad \Rightarrow \quad H^* = 0 \qquad (2.1)$$

where U_L is the partial derivative of U with respect to L, μ is the Lagrange multiplier. From equation (2.1), we can see that the decision of whether to work depends on the comparison between market wage rate and one's reservation wage. ① Reservation wage depends on one's tastes for work, and other factors, such as non-labor income. ② If the market wage rate is below the reservation

---

① Reservation wage is the slope of one's indifference curve at the endowment point if depicted graphically.

② If we assume leisure is normal good, the increase in non-labor income will increase reservation wage.

wage, the individual will choose not to work.

Theoretical effect of market wage on labor force participation is always positive, unlike the ambiguous predictions in the case of positive working hours. It is because for a person with zero working hours, rise in wage will generate no income effect. Therefore, increasing female real wage along with declining labor force participation rate over the sample years implies the reservation wage are increasing at an even faster rate. Theoretical predicted effect of non-labor income is negative for both decisions of participation and hours to work.

2.4.2 Empirical Model

To estimate the participation function, I use the following empirical specification [equation (2.2)], which is yielded by the static labor supply theory. The hypothesis of constant coefficient during the whole sample period is tested using Likelihood Ratio Test, and is decisively rejected. Therefore, I estimate separate participation function for each sample year.① The regressors include wage, non-labor income and demographic characteristics (education level, age, family structure, etc.), which are determinants used in the traditional empirical literature:

$$P_{it} = \alpha_{0t} + \alpha_{1t} \ln W_{it} + \alpha_{2t} \ln V_{it} + \gamma'_t X_{it} + \epsilon_{it} \quad (2.2)$$

And its Probit version is:

$$P^*_{it} = \beta_{0t} + \beta_{1t} \ln W_{it} + \beta_{2t} \ln V_{it} + \delta'_t X_{it} + \varepsilon_{it}$$

$$P_{it} = \begin{cases} 1 & \text{if } P^*_{it} > 0 \\ 0 & \text{Otherise} \end{cases}$$

where in equation (2.2), P_{it} is the participation indicator, which is a dummy variable equals 1 if individual i participates in the labor force in year t and equals 0 if not (t = 1988, 1995, 2002, or 2007). W_{it} denotes individual i's own annual real wage income (including imputed annual wage for the non-

---

① Coefficients are subscripted with t to indicate that the equation is estimated for each sample year.

participants and participants with invalid wage data) in year t. V_{it} is the non-labor income, which includes household property income (interest, dividend, rent) plus husband's earnings for married women. X_{it} contains other variables affecting labor participation decision, including age, age square, education dummies, co-residence status with children under 15, co-residence status with parents older than 60, husband's age, square of husband's age, province dummies and number of household members. ϵ_{it} is the disturbance term. In this traditional static labor supply function, α_{1t} measures the effect of uncompensated wage change, while α_{2t} indicates the income effect.

2.4.3 Econometric Issues

Before estimating the above empirical specification for each sample year, I need to discuss several econometric issues commonly confronted: methods of imputing wages to non-participants and the possible endogeneity problem associated with the wage variable.

1. Imputation of Wages for Non-participants

In order to recover the full distribution of offered wages instead of focusing on the censored one of accepted wages, and to estimate the participation function, potential market wage rate for non-participants has to be imputed. To offset the impact of selection bias, several methods have been proposed in the existing literature.

One of the commonly used method is suggested by Juhn (1992), which is to impute wage for non-workers based on the wage distribution of the workers who worked 1 – 13 weeks per year. She first divides the data into race-experience-education cells, and then weights each worker who worked 1 – 13 weeks by $(N_0 + N_{1-13})/(N_{1-13})$, where N_0 and N_{1-13} are the number of people who did not work and who had worked 1 – 13 weeks in that cell in that specific year. This method is similar to the method of "Matching Cell Mean", while taking into account the people in a specific cell without observed wages and assuming the wage distribution of non-workers is the same with the workers who worked 1 – 13 weeks. Another method under the similar assumption is described in Juhn (1991), which is to impute wage of non-workers according to the wage distribution observed. Based on the same assumption on the resemblance between non-workers and people who worked for 1 – 13 weeks, a non-worker is assigned with a vector of 10 probabilities, each of them corresponding to the relative frequency of 1 – 13 weeks workers in a specific wage decile; the corresponding wage is the mean wage of that wage decile. In other words, each non-worker contributes to 10 observations in this method. Blau and Kahn (2005) also take this assumption, but they use wage regression instead of the nonparametric approach used by Juhn.①Unfortunately, although this method has been widely used while dealing with the CPS data, the number of working weeks last year can only be inferred for the 1995 and 2002 CHIPS data. Also, the information on working weeks throughout the year is not directly and consistently asked in all surveys. Thus, this imputing method cannot be adopted for our data.

Due to the coarseness of the data, I use the imputation method suggested by Blau and Beller (1992)②, which is essentially the combination of "Matching Cell Mean" and "Adjustment Factors". Particularly, they assume the potential wage for a non-participant is less than a participant with similar observed qualities, and this difference is due to their disparities in unobserved characteristics. Therefore, for the wage imputation of non-participants, they use regression matching, and then apply adjustment factors (such as 0.6 or 0.8) to account

---

① Separate wage regressions are performed for each "year-gender-weeks worked (less than 20 weeks or 20 and higher)" combination. Besides the non-workers, people with invalid wage information also received imputed wages according to their weeks worked. The regressors included in the wage regression are own and spouse's variables for age, age squared, three education categories, the race categories, and eight region categories.

② Methods suggested by Brown and Beller (1984) is similar with Blau and Beller (1992) in the sense that he also assumes the potential wages for non-participants are less than participants with the same measured characteristics. This idea is implemented by assuming that the potential wages offered to non-participants come from random draw below the median of observed wages distribution.

for that difference. Furthermore, this idea has been empirically confirmed by Juhn (1992). She uses the cross-section CPS data and shows that there is evidence for a well-ordered positive relationship between participation weeks and wages for workers with the same education and experience level as shown in Table V in her paper.

Specifically, I divide the data into 102 groups (wage cells) based on education level, potential experience and sample year. Particularly, for education level, there are 3 categories: middle school and below, high school and tech and university and above; for potential experience, I divide it using 5 – year interval and 10 categories are generated in total; for sample year, there are 4 of them in total (t = 1988, 1995, 2002, 2007). Then, I calculate the mean of the real wage income for the workers falling into each wage cell. To get the full wage distribution $f_t(w)$, I impute wage for nonparticipants by multiplying the mean wage of the wage cell she belongs to by the adjustment factor of 0.8, and use the mean wage of her cell directly for participants with invalid wage data (Blau, 2007). After imputing wage for the people without valid wage data, the full distribution of offered wage is recovered. [1]

Another traditional method to correct the selection bias is proposed by Heckman (1979), which involves simultaneous estimation of the participation equation and the wage equation. However, this approach is often accused of being unstable and greatly depending on the model specification and the specific dataset. Therefore, I use this imputation method as robustness check. Specifically, for each sample year, I first estimate the reduced form Probit participation function; then estimate the selection corrected wage equation by including inverse Mills ratio calculated from the first step. The exclusion of non-labor income and co-reside status with children under 15 years old in the wage equation provides identification condition for the inverse Mills ratio. In the third step, I generate a predicted

---

[1] For the treatment of outlier, I drop the observations whose logarithm of real income is beyond or below the outer fences of the logarithm of real income by year.

wage from the wage regression, and the corresponding values are imputed for the non-participants or people with invalid wage data. ① The results using the method proposed by Heckman are similar to the main results reported in this paper.

2. Endogeneity of Wage

(1) Measurement Error.

Measurement error in the wage variable is another issue needed to be discussed when estimating the labor supply elasticity. As pointed out by Borjas (1980), the conventional method of calculating the wage rate by dividing annual (or weekly) wage earnings by annual (or weekly) working hours leads to a downward bias, as long as there is measurement error in the labor supply measure. This bias is caused by the fact that the hours worked appears in both sides of the equation, and it is widely known as division bias. One correcting method is to find a proxy for the hourly wage variable by estimating the wage function and using predicted hourly wage instead for each individual in the sample. However, this approach is unstable and sensitive to the choice of the variables in the hours equation. Nevertheless, in my estimation of the participation function, this division bias is less important because hours worked is not used as the dependent variable and the annual wage income is employed as the regressors.

The standard approach is to find instrument variables for the hourly wage variable, which requires examining the dataset very carefully. For example, Borjas (1980) suggests to use "hours worked last week" as the hours measure to compute the wage rate while still using the usual hours as the dependent variable (cross-division). Or, the lagged usual wage rate can be used for the longitudinal dataset. For example, Blundell and MaCurdy (1999) suggest the lagged observed wage can be used as a valid instrument if the measurement error is serially

---

① The explanatory variables in the wage regression include a cubic of potential experience, education dummies and provincial dummies; the explanatory variables in the first-step reduced form participation equation includes the above regressors plus the non-labor income and co-reside status with children under 15 years old.

uncorrelated. Additionally, as in Blau and Kahn (2005), a series of dummy variables indicating the decile of own and spouse's wages can be used as the excluded instruments.

Juhn (1992) uses two methods to address the issue of measurement error. One method is to adjust the difference between the transformation of the inverse cumulative wage distribution for the wage of last year and the wage of the survey week. This method reduces the measurement error to its level of the survey week. Her data show that the difference between those two wage measures is larger for the extreme percentiles. Another method is to use education as the instrumental variable for wages, and estimate the participation function using the variations in wages and the participation rate among different education groups.

(2) Omitted Variables.

Some unobservable characteristics, such as motivation, may affect both people's willingness to participate in the labor market and the wage offer she gets. The instrumental approach and the grouped method (Angrist, 1991) can be used to address this issue. In Juhn (1992), she also mentions this problem and refers to another source of variation (regional time series) as a way of solution.

2.4.4 Results

I estimate the equation (2.2) and its Probit version for each sample year. [①] Sample statistics are shown in Table 2.2. Results gained from the Linear Probability model and the Probit model show that all coefficients estimates are expected from the theory predictions in terms of both coefficient signs and significance level. The explanatory variables included in the regressions can be approximately divided into four categories: women's own wage rate, household non-labor

---

[①] The results obtained from the Linear Probability model are reported in Table 2.3, and the results gained from the Probit model are reported in Table 2.6 in Appendix B.

income, variables representing women's human capital and variables describing women's family structure. Their effects on female labor market participation will be discussed in turn.

Firstly, static labor supply theory emphasizes greatly on the role of wage in explaining labor supply behavior, and predicts unambiguous positive wage participation elasticity. This positive wage effect on female participation decision is confirmed in my estimates. The signs of the coefficients of the wage variable are positive and significant throughout, indicating a rise in wage will increase the probability of participation. No trend has been detected for the wage participation elasticity in the LPM results, but an increasing trend in the magnitude of the wage coefficient is found in the Probit estimates. Secondly, non-labor income exerts negative influence on women's propensities to participate. The LPM estimates suggest the coefficients of the non-labor income variable have become significant since 2002 and its magnitude has been increasing substantially over the sample period, indicating non-labor income plays a bigger role in women's participation decisions in recent years. Thirdly, the coefficients associated with education level are significant at the conventional levels and correct in signs for most of the sample years. For the education dummies, the category "University and above" serves as the base group. Thus, the negative signs for the coefficients of "Middle school and below" and "High school and tech" indicate the people with lower education level are less likely to participate in the labor force. In addition, education's positive effect on participation tends to increase over the years, meaning human capital factors are becoming an increasingly important determinant of female labor supply. The coefficients of the women's age variable and its square are also significant throughout. Lastly, the results suggest the presence of younger children in a family negatively affects the labor force participation decisions of married women, and this negative effect shows marked increasing magnitude over the years. Family size has a positive impact on women's labor force participation decisions and the estimates of its coefficients are significant in most of the sample periods.

Table 2.3   Estimates of the Participation Functions (LPM)

	(1) 1988	(2) 1995	(3) 2002	(4) 2007
Wage	0.0893 *** (0.00)	0.1021 *** (0.00)	0.0522 *** (0.00)	0.0893 *** (0.00)
Non-labor income	-0.0019 (0.87)	-0.0277 * (0.04)	-0.0324 * (0.02)	-0.0831 *** (0.00)
Age	0.0709 *** (0.00)	0.1043 *** (0.00)	0.1307 *** (0.00)	0.1206 *** (0.00)
Age square	-0.1093 *** (0.00)	-0.1586 *** (0.00)	-0.1816 *** (0.00)	-0.1730 *** (0.00)
Middle school and below	-0.1053 *** (0.00)	-0.1024 *** (0.00)	-0.1178 *** (0.00)	-0.1613 *** (0.00)
High school and tech	-0.0595 ** (0.00)	-0.0695 * (0.02)	-0.0138 (0.66)	-0.0762 (0.05)
Co-reside with children under 15	-0.0372 *** (0.00)	-0.0519 *** (0.00)	-0.0818 *** (0.00)	-0.1048 *** (0.00)
Co-reside with parents (60+)	-0.0236 * (0.04)	-0.0045 (0.83)	0.0059 (0.82)	0.0358 (0.42)
Husband's age	0.0176 ** (0.01)	0.0009 (0.95)	0.0319 (0.06)	0.0240 (0.31)
Husband's age square	-0.0191 * (0.01)	0.0012 (0.93)	-0.0435 * (0.02)	-0.0319 (0.25)
Number of household member	0.0159 *** (0.00)	0.0253 ** (0.00)	0.0042 (0.70)	0.0315 (0.09)
Constant	-1.0533 *** (0.00)	-1.2119 *** (0.00)	-1.9630 *** (0.00)	-1.5582 *** (0.00)
Observations	3 648	2 141	1 996	962
Adjusted R-squared	0.309	0.355	0.359	0.258

Note: Wage of the non-workers is imputed using Adjusted Matching Cell Mean. All the models also include provincial dummies, which are not reported in this table. Linear Probability model is used.

* significant at 5%, ** significant at 1%, *** significant at 0.1%.

2.5 Accounting for the Changes in Female Labor Force Participation in Urban China

The estimation of the participation functions quantifies the effects of both demand-side and supply-side factors for each sample year, and the results are in accordance with the theoretical predictions. To further investigate the driving forces of the change in female LFPR over time, I conduct decomposition analysis based on the estimation results of the participation functions, in the attempt to systematically relate the decline in labor participation to the socio-economic changes happening in China during the same period. Particularly, in this section, I try to explore to what extent this general decline in female LFPR can be explained by the change in the distribution of the population variables in the economy, i.e. characteristic effects; and to what extent it associates with the change in the behavioral pattern, i.e. coefficient effects. I use both linear and non-linear decomposition techniques to conduct the accounting analysis.

2.5.1 Previous Studies

The decomposition approach has been used to study the change in labor force participation rate over time in many previous studies. Gomulka and Stern (1990) investigate the increasing trend in female employment rate in the United Kingdom using a Probit model and a time-series of the cross-sections data from the Family Expenditure Survey (FES). They propose a framework of growth accounting in this paper. Specifically, they first estimate a model of employment on the annual cross-section data, and then construct a 13 × 13 matrix based on the estimation of the employment models.[1] In each row of the matrix, the employment ratio of a

---

[1] The period they studied is from 1970 to 1982, which includes 13 years in total.

specific sample is estimated using the coefficients from the estimation of every year; while for each column, the estimates from a specific year is used to estimate all the samples from 1970 – 1982. Their results show that most of the increase in employment rate during the sample period could be accounted for by the change in coefficients. To further investigate which coefficient contributes the most, the authors use the constant sample and the coefficients associated with that sample (except for the coefficient to be investigated) to isolate the effect of that specific coefficient. Changes in the distribution of specific population characteristics have also been investigated. After the seminal work of Gomulka and Stern (1990), Gutiérrez-Domenech and Bell (2004) also use this growth accounting framework to study the labor force participation trend in the United Kingdom using the same dataset, with minor changes in the method of estimating the contribution of specific population characteristics to the overall change in LFPR.

Juhn (1992) uses the decomposition framework which focuses on the changing distribution of the wage variable, and the micro data from the Current Population Surveys to analyze the decline in labor force participation among prime-age men in the U.S. from 1967 to 1987. Descriptive analysis shows that the decline in labor force participation happens mostly in the less educated group and men with lower earnings potential, and the wage structure changes in a similar way in the United States during the same period. Therefore, Juhn (1992) proposes a decomposition framework focusing on the wage variable, which aims to systematically relate the two phenomena, and especially to analyze how much of the decline in male labor force participation could be explained by the change in market opportunities. The decomposition framework in her paper is characterized by the following equation:

$$P_t - P_{t'} = \int p_t(w) f_t(w) dw - \int p_{t'}(w) f_{t'}(w) dw$$

$$= \int p_{t'}(w) [f_t(w) - f_{t'}(w)] dw$$

$$+ \int [p_t(w) - p_{t'}(w)] f_t(w) dw \quad (2.3)$$

where $p_t(w)$ describes the participation behavior of a typical individual at time t; $f_t(w)$ is the distribution of offered wages at time t; $P_t = \int p_t(w) f_t(w) dw$ represents the aggregate participation rate at time t; and equation (2.3) is the change in the aggregate labor force participation rate between time t' and t. The decomposition suggests that two potential sources could attribute to the change in the aggregate labor force participation rate: the change in market opportunity (demand), which could be represented by the shift in $f_t(w)$; and the change in non-market opportunities (supply), which could be represented by the shift in $p_t(w)$. After estimating the wage offer distribution $f_t(w)$ and the participation function $p_t(w)$, the author compares the plots of $f_t(w)$ and $p_t(w)$ from different sample periods and conducts accounting analysis. She reaches the conclusion that the change in wage structure could account for most of the decrease in male LFPR from the early 1970s through the late 1980s, while the supply-side factors dominate in explaining the initial decline from the late 1960s to the early 1970s.

Blau and Kahn (2005) also use a similar decomposition technique to investigate the labor supply behavior at the intensive margin for married women from 1980 to 2000. Specifically, they use the IV approach and find that both of their own wage elasticity and cross wage elasticity are drastically declining during the sample period. Following the regression, the accounting analysis has been conducted to investigate the relative importance of the changes in explanatory variables and the shifts in the labor supply function in explaining the total changes in married women's unconditional annual work hours. The results suggest a large rightward shift in their labor supply function in the 1980s and very little shift in the 1990s. For the detailed decomposition, the increase in real wage contributes most to the rise in labor supply.

2.5.2 Decomposition Framework

Based on the estimates obtained from the Linear Probability model and the

Probit model, the change in female labor force participation can be decomposed into the part associated with the change in social-demographic characteristics, and the part arising from the change in the participation behavior or in the unobserved or omitted relevant factors. The latter part are reflected by the change in the coefficients of each year's participation function, and are commonly referred to as coefficient effects. The standard Blinder-Oaxaca Decomposition and its extensions to limited dependent variable models by Fairlie (2005) are discussed as the methods for linear and non-linear decomposition.

1. Linear Decomposition

The standard Blinder-Oaxaca decomposition framework can be used for the regression results obtained by the Linear Probability Model. Using this method, the mean outcome difference can be decomposed into the differences in characteristics (explained part) and residual difference (unexplained part). Specifically, the change in labor force participation rate during the year t and the year $t + 1$ is decomposed as:

$$\bar{P}_t - \bar{P}_{t+1} = [\bar{X}_t - \bar{X}_{t+1}]'\beta^* + [\bar{X}_t'(\beta_t - \beta^*) + \bar{X}_{t+1}'(\beta^* - \beta_{t+1})] \tag{2.4}$$

where $\bar{P}_t$ is the labor force participation rate in the year t; X_t contains all the regressors included in the linear probability regression; β^* is the coefficients from the pooled regression using the data of the years t and $t+1$; β_t is the coefficients from the regression of the year t. The first component amounts to the differential that is due to the group differences in the explanatory variables, while the second component measures the unexplained part. Estimation of the sampling variance follows the methods proposed by Jann (2008).

To further disintegrate the overall explained part into the contributions of the change in each specific explanatory variable, detailed decomposition can also be performed. In the detailed decomposition, I focus on the contributions of the changing distributions in wage, non-labor income, age, education, and co-residency with children under 15 years old, since the coefficients of these variables are statistically significant for most of the sample years as shown in the regression results. Therefore, the contributions of those five population changes are mainly assessed in the latter part of this paper. It should be noted though, due to the difficulty of interpretation, I focus on the explained part of the decomposition, following most of the previous studies using this technique. For the unexplained part, detailed decomposition results have meaningful interpretation only for the variables with natural zero point, i.e, arbitrary scaling is not allowed (Jones and Kelley, 1984).

2. Non-linear Decomposition

If the participation function is estimated using the Probit model or the Logit model instead of the Linear Probability model, non-linear decomposition technique needs to be adopted. Based on the extension proposed by Fairlie (2005), in this case, the decomposition for the change in LFPR between the year t and the year $t+1$ can be performed using the following equation[①]:

$$\bar{P}_t - \bar{P}_{t+1} = \left[\sum_{i=1}^{N_t} \frac{F(X_{it}\hat{\beta}_t)}{N_t} - \sum_{i=1}^{N_{t+1}} \frac{F(X_{i,t+1}\hat{\beta}_t)}{N_{t+1}} \right]$$
$$+ \left[\sum_{i=1}^{N_{t+1}} \frac{F(X_{i,t+1}\hat{\beta}_t)}{N_{t+1}} - \sum_{i=1}^{N_{t+1}} \frac{F(X_{i,t+1}\hat{\beta}_{t+1})}{N_{t+1}} \right] \quad (2.5)$$

where the first bracketed term in the right hand side stands for the change associated with the group difference in the distributions of X between two years, and the second term corresponds to the change arising from the difference in the coefficients in two year's participation functions.

Detailed decomposition is more complicated than overall decomposition in the non-linear case. The basic idea is to hold the distribution of the other variables constant while changing the distribution of the interested variable, and then calculate the change in average predicted probability.[②] Standard errors are calculated using the delta method.

[①] Different weights can be applied. For instance, $\hat{\beta}_{t+1}$ for the first term, and the year t distribution of the independent variables for the second term.

[②] Further details could be found in Fairlie (2005).

2.5.3 Results

The specification used in the regression model has also been adopted for the decomposition analysis. All the regressors are included, even for those which are not significant in some of the sample periods. The purpose is to give the explanatory variables their best chances to account for the differential in LFPR between the studied years. More parsimonious version has been tried and similar results are gained. The main findings of the decomposition analysis suggest that between 1988 and 1995, changes in age structure and household size contribute to the decline in the female labor participation. Between 1995 and 2002, both changes in age structure and non-labor income contribute. Between 2002 and 2007, increasing non-labor income can explain most part of the decline. I obtain similar results using non-linear de-composition technique and the results gained from non-linear decomposition are reported in Table 2.7 of Appendix B.

Table 2.4 shows the linear decomposition results. ①For the overall decomposition, the change in endowments cannot explain the decline in LFPR between 1988 – 1995 and between 2002 – 2007, suggesting the declines during those two periods are mostly driven by the changes in participation behavior, i.e. the leftward shifted labor supply function. Between 1995 – 2002, nearly 18.6% of the decline could be accounted by the difference in measured characteristics.

Table 2.4 Linear Decomposition of Labor Force Participation Rate (%)

	1988 – 1995		1995 – 2002		2002 – 2007	
	Coef.	% of Diff.	Coef.	% of Diff.	Coef.	% of Diff.
Overall decomposition						
Observed change	–4.82		–5.32		–5.49	
Contribution from endowments	1.23		–0.99		2.58	
Contribution from coefficients	–6.06		–4.33		–8.07	

---

① Reported results are weighted by the coefficients from the pooled regression. Different sets of weights have been tried and the main results remain robust.

continued

	1988 – 1995		1995 – 2002		2002 – 2007	
	Coef.	% of Diff.	Coef.	% of Diff.	Coef.	% of Diff.
Detailed decomposition (explained)						
Demand						
Wage	2.27 (0.00)	-47.0%	2.37 (0.00)	-44.6%	4.16 (0.00)	-75.8%
Supply						
Non-labor income	-0.51 (0.07)	10.6%	-0.95 (0.01)	17.8%	-2.68 (0.00)	48.9%
Age	-1.06 (0.01)	22.1%	-3.90 (0.00)	73.4%	-0.11 (0.88)	2.1%
Education	0.62 (0.00)	-12.9%	0.92 (0.00)	-17.4%	0.84 (0.00)	-15.3%
Co-reside with children under 15	0.56 (0.00)	-11.6%	0.88 (0.00)	-16.5%	0.21 (0.25)	-3.8%
Family size	-0.80 (0.00)	16.6%	-0.15 (0.12)	2.8%	-0.06 (0.35)	1.0%

Source: Author's Calculations using Chinese Household Income Project Series.

Although the overall decomposition does not tell us so much about the sources of the decline, it would still be meaningful to look at the relative contribution of the change in specific population characteristics. Particularly, from 1988 to 1995, aging accounts for 22.1% of the total decline in LFPR, while decreasing family size accounts for 16.6%; from 1995 to 2002, aging dominates and contributes 73.4%, while rising non-labor income explains 17.8% of the actual decline; from 2002 to 2007, increasing non-labor income dominates and accounts for 48.9% of the actual decline. Therefore, by quantifying the characteristics contribution for each explanatory variable, the decomposition results indicate the changing distribution of age structure and non-labor income in China over the sample years are two of the most important population changes contributing to the decline in female labor force participation.

It is in line with the demographic transition happening in China during the same period. Due to the One-Child policy which was implemented in 1979, China's population is quickly aging. It is also reflected in the age composition of our sample.① The aging of the population is also confirmed by other data sources. For instance, *China Compendium of Statistics* suggests the population's natural growth rate has decreased dramatically during 1988 – 2007, from 15.73% in 1988 to 5.17% in 2007.

Demographic changes influence the aggregate labor force participation rate because of the life-cycle patterns of labor force participation. Quite interestingly, the change in China's age structure resembles the recent aging population structure in the U.S.. In the U.S., this rising share of older people results from the aging baby-boom cohort who were born between 1946 and 1964.② Additionally, starting from the beginning of the 21st century, the female labor force participation rate in the U.S. has shown a decreasing trend, and this reversal pattern of female labor supply has been investigated from the angle of demographic changes as well (Aaronson et al., 2006).

Increasing non-labor income also contributes significantly to this declining trend in female LFPR, and plays an increasingly vital role over time. The static labor supply theory suggests that the increase in non-labor income will decrease labor force participation through income effect. Shown in our data, the real non-labor income for married women has increased from ￥2 032 to ￥9 501 during 1988 – 2007. Especially during 2002 – 2007, it has more than doubled from

---

① For the 2007 CHIPS dataset which is now publicly available, the sampling method is not consistent with the former three waves, thus it is of limited use when it comes to the analysis regarding the changing population age structure. More details of this issue are discussed in the last section of this paper. Moreover, it should also be noted that I have excluded employers and self-employed individuals, which could also affect the age structure of the sample.

② In China, having more children was encouraged by the government until the 1960s.

¥4 538 to ¥9 501. ①Thus, the evolution of non-labor income over the sample years is also consistent with the patterns detected in the decomposition results.

Considering the lack in explaining power from population changes overall, there must exist social-economic transitions offsetting the above effects, at least to some extent. There are mainly three of them: increasing female real wage, rising female education level, and declining proportion of women who co-reside with their children under 15 years old. These changes also happen in developed countries, and are often being used to explain the upward trend in female LFPR in developed countries over the last century. However, in China's case, while the participation effects of these variables are still consistent with the theoretical predictions and the empirical evidence gained by other economic literature, their contributions have clearly been mitigated by the changes in population age structure and non-labor income.

Of these offsetting population changes, the contributions of rising female real wage are significant and the largest in magnitude for all the sample periods. Moreover, wage effect appears to increase over time. My sample calculation also shows that female real wage rose more in the later periods. ② Compared with the wage variable, education effect on the movement of participation rate exhibits similar patterns but with smaller magnitudes. The education effects are slightly larger for the later years as well. In Table 2.2, we can also observe this drastic increase in women's education level over the sample years. For instance, the proportion of women with university and above degree in 2007 is more than

---

① Based on the exchange rate on April 2016, 1 Chinese Yuan approximately equals 0.15 US Dollar.

② Based on author's calculations using the CHIPS dataset, in 1988, female real wage income was ¥1 589.8, this number rose to ¥2 135.5 in 1995, ¥3 355.6 in 2002 and ¥6 621.8 in 2007. It should be noted though, despite the rapid increase in female real wage, the gender wage gap has been widening up over the sample years as well. After restricting sample to be the people with valid information for wage income and adjusting it using the spatial price indices, I find the female/male ratio of real wage income has been decreasing during the sample period, from 0.81 in 1988 to 0.75 in 2007, which is in contrast with the trend observed in the United States. In the U.S., the increasing trend in female/male ratio of annual earnings is documented by many literature (Blau and Kahn, 2005). Widening gender wage gap will discourage female labor force participation.

four times of that proportion in the year 1988. Lastly, changes in the proportion of women co-residing with children under 15 years old also have significant negative contributions in two periods.

However, decomposition analysis is certainly the mere first step to disentangle the mystery of declining female labor force participation nowadays in China for its own limitations. Firstly, this method is similar as growth accounting, which does not help us to identify the underlying causal relationship between the involved variables. Secondly, the change which is unexplained by the population changes can also be due to the differences in unobserved population characteristics or the relevant factors which are not captured by our regression model. Thirdly, due to the technical issues, such as the lack of natural zero point, it is usually difficult, if not impossible, to distinguish the group membership and the difference in coefficients for the unexplained part (Jones and Kelley, 1984). Fourthly, the decomposition results can be biased estimates if the evolution of the characteristics is not truly exogenous, but is in response to the change in the coefficients over the years (Gutiérrez-Domenech and Bell, 2004).

2.6 Conclusion

This chapter uses the Chinese Household Income Project Series from 1988 to 2007 to study the declining female labor force participation rate in China since the late 1980s. The participation functions have been estimated for each sample year, and the regression results are consistent with the theoretical predictions of the static labor supply model. Based on that, the changes in female labor participation during the periods studied have been decomposed into the changes due to the difference in observable characteristics and the changes due to the difference in coefficients. Following most of the studies using decomposition technique, the contributions of changes in population characteristics have been focused.

Decomposition results suggest that although the increase in wage and education level, together with the decrease in the proportion of married women co-residing with their younger children, have all contributed to an increasing trend in female labor participation rate, their effects have been dominated by the changes in age and non-labor income distribution during the same time. The results indicate that the government should loosen the population control policy to slow down the speed of aging in nowadays China. Besides, it is also recommendable for the government to further develop the service sector and to promote the information technology revolution, in order to influence the wage structure and to enhance the effect of changing wage distribution.

It should be noted though, due to the limitations of the 2007 dataset, the decomposition results of the period 2002 – 2007 may not well reflect the effect of changing population age distribution. More details about the data limitations are discussed in Appendix C. Also, the potential endogeneity problems associated with the wage and non-labor variables have not been taken care of using traditional instrumental variable approach, because the main purpose of this paper is to account for the movement in LFPR over time, and also because the LPM and the Probit model give relative consistent results with the theoretical predictions and other empirical evidence. Therefore, the simple modeling methods are used to increase transparency.

Another interesting finding of this chapter is the growing importance of non-labor income in explaining the change in female labor supply. At the more aggregate level, a U-shaped female labor force participation rate over the path of economic growth has been pointed out in many economic literature and Feminization U hypothesis has been proposed. Particularly, Feminization U hypothesis contends the initial decline in female labor supply can be caused by the fact that the substitution effect has been dominated by the income effect at earlier stage of economic development. It is indeed the trend I find in this chapter. Therefore, to explain the continuing decreasing trend in female labor force participation rate, a comparison between the wage effect and non-labor income effect would be an interesting angle to pursue after I gain more data after 2007.

2.7 Appendix

Appendix A: Variable Construction

1. Participation

In 1988 Survey, nonparticipation is defined as those who are disabled, or retired, or currently students, or waiting to enter school, or homemakers doing housework, or in other situations, or do not know, among those who received income in 1988 but are not currently employed. If neither of these cases is true, the person is defined as a participant. In 1995 Survey, nonparticipation is defined as those who are retired, or full-time students, or full-time homemakers, or pre-school children, or disabled injured or had chronic disease, or unable to work, or in other situations. If a person belongs to the categories other than the above ones, she/he is defined as a participant. In 2002 Survey, nonparticipation is defined as those who are officially off-duty (*Lixiu*), or retired, or unable to work, or early retirement, or the youth waiting for job assignment, or full-time homemakers, or full-time students, or waiting for job assignment or entering a higher school, or in other situations. [1] If a person belongs to the categories other than the above ones, she/he is defined as a participant. In 2007 Survey, nonparticipation is defined as those who are retired, household workers, lost capacity to work, in school students/preschool children, awaiting job assignment/com-

---

[1] The definition of "unemployed" used in the 2002 CHIPS codebook encompasses individuals who are without a job and seeking employment, including those who have been laid off (*xiagang*), having taken early retirement, or are off-post (*ligang*).

mencement of further education/withdrawn from studies, or in other situations. If a person belongs to the categories other than the above ones, she/he is defined as a participant.

2. Wage

In 1988 Survey, monthly wage income is defined as the sum of regular wage, floating wage, contract income, all kinds of bonuses/above-quota wages, all kinds of subsidies, other wages, other cash income from work unit, hardship allowance, and other working income. Annual wage income is computed as monthly income times 12, since they are reported as monthly average in 1988 Survey. Information on working hours is not reported this year. In 1995 Survey, annual wage income is computed as the sum of wages, other income from the work unit, income of employees of individual enterprise, other employee income, and other income generated from labour, since I focus on the group of people engaged in wage employment. Annual work hour is computed as the product of average number of work days per week, actual number of work hours on an average day and 52 weeks. In 2002 Survey, annual wage income includes wage and subsidy, and other income from work. Annual work hour is computed as the product of employed months, working days per month, and average hours per working day. In 2007 Survey, monthly wage income is computed as average monthly income from the current primary job or from all the jobs with pay if the interviewee has other part-time jobs besides the current primary job. Wage income is not directly asked in the survey, but in the instructions to the question regarding average monthly income, it specifies that for the wage earner, income refers to wages, bonuses, allowances and commutations in-kind. Annual work hour is calculated as the product of average working hours per week and 52 weeks a year in the similar manner.

Appendix B: Other Descriptive and Estimation Results

Table 2.5 Female Labor Force Participation Rate by Age and Education (1988 – 2007)

	Age Group							
	16 – 19	20 – 24	25 – 29	30 – 34	35 – 39	40 – 44	45 – 49	50 – 55
1988								
Middle school and below	0.973	0.991	1.000	0.997	0.991	0.985	0.900	0.401
High school and tech	0.977	1.000	0.997	0.998	1.000	1.000	0.972	0.805
University and above	1.000	1.000	1.000	1.000	1.000	1.000	1.000	0.964
1995								
Middle school and below	0.885	0.985	0.918	0.967	0.956	0.948	0.725	0.285
High school and tech	0.922	0.990	0.977	0.997	0.988	0.992	0.876	0.505
University and above		1.000	1.000	1.000	1.000	1.000	0.867	0.882
2002								
Middle school and below		0.647	0.763	0.960	0.893	0.915	0.760	0.190
High school and tech		0.979	0.953	1.000	0.949	0.980	0.897	0.509
University and above		0.889	0.964	1.000	1.000	1.000	0.929	0.667
2007								
Middle school and below			0.478	0.737	0.853	0.820	0.671	0.213
High school and tech		0.842	0.878	0.926	0.877	0.889	0.801	0.311
University and above		0.867	0.907	0.982	1.000	1.000	0.917	0.688

Source: Author's Calculations using Chinese Household Income Project Series.

Table 2.6 Estimates of the Participation Functions (Probit) (1988 – 2007)

	(1) 1988	(2) 1995	(3) 2002	(4) 2007
Wage	0.0120 ** (0.00)	0.0505 *** (0.00)	0.0470 *** (0.00)	0.1148 *** (0.00)
Non-labor income	0.0027 (0.23)	– 0.0096 (0.32)	– 0.0225 (0.08)	– 0.0883 *** (0.00)

continued

	(1) 1988	(2) 1995	(3) 2002	(4) 2007
Age	0.0024 (0.22)	0.0241 (0.08)	0.0904 *** (0.00)	0.1015 *** (0.00)
Age square	-0.0046 (0.06)	-0.0409 ** (0.01)	-0.1229 *** (0.00)	-0.1440 *** (0.00)
Middle school and below (d)	-0.0198 (0.08)	-0.1090 * (0.02)	-0.1731 * (0.01)	-0.2736 ** (0.00)
High school and tech (d)	-0.0157 (0.31)	-0.0644 (0.07)	-0.0618 (0.14)	-0.1368 ** (0.01)
Co-reside with children under 15 (d)	0.0046 (0.09)	0.0017 (0.88)	-0.0422 (0.05)	-0.0899 * (0.02)
Husband's age	0.0020 (0.18)	-0.0021 (0.87)	0.0073 (0.68)	0.0200 (0.43)
Husband's age square	-0.0023 (0.13)	0.0028 (0.83)	-0.0143 (0.45)	-0.0270 (0.36)
Number of household member	-0.0004 (0.42)	0.0097 (0.05)	0.0025 (0.78)	0.0522 ** (0.01)
Observations	3 648	2 141	1 996	962

Note: Marginal effects; p-values in parentheses. (d) for discrete change of dummy variable from 0 to 1. Wage of the non-workers is imputed using Adjusted Matching Cell Mean. All the models also include provincial dummies, which are not reported in this table. Probit model is used.

* significant at 5%, ** significant at 1%, *** significant at 0.1%.

Table 2.7 Non-linear Decomposition of Labor Force Participation Rate (%)

	1988 - 1995		1995 - 2002		2002 - 2007	
	Coef.	% of Diff.	Coef.	% of Diff.	Coef.	% of Diff.
Overall decomposition						
Observed change	-4.82		-5.32		-5.49	
Contribution from endowments	0.15		-2.05	0.38	3.67	

continued

	1988 – 1995		1995 – 2002		2002 – 2007	
	Coef.	% of Diff.	Coef.	% of Diff.	Coef.	% of Diff.
Detailed decomposition (explained)						
Demand						
Wage	0.62 (0.02)	–13%	1.54 (0.00)	–29%	5.04 (0.00)	–92%
Supply						
Non-labor income	–0.12 (0.62)	3%	–0.51 (0.08)	10%	–2.62 (0.00)	48%
Age	–0.27 (0.59)	6%	–3.67 (0.00)	69%	–0.23 (0.69)	4%
Education	0.37 (0.01)	–8%	0.98 (0.00)	–18%	1.03 (0.00)	–19%
Co-reside with children under 15	–0.17 (0.27)	3%	0.22 (0.24)	–4%	0.12 (0.40)	–2%
Family size	–0.26 (0.19)	5%	–0.10 (0.50)	2%	–0.06 (0.31)	1%

Source: Author's Calculations using Chinese Household Income Project Series.

Appendix C: Limitations of the Data

Although the CHIPS is a relatively authoritative data source for the study of China's labor market, it should be noted that the CHIPS 2007 has certain limitations for the comparative study due to its different sampling method. The CHIPS 1988 – 2002 draw their samples from significantly large samples used by the National Bureau of Statistics of China (NBS); while the urban data of CHIPS 2007 consists of two parts: the 10 000 urban household data from the large samples of the NBS, which are nationally representative, and the 5 000 urban household data from 9 provinces, which was designed to supplement the NBS data.

The CHIPS 2007 used in this chapter is the latter 5 000 household sample based on the CHIPS questionnaire, since the 10 000 urban household data has not yet been released to public use until the date this paper was written. Even though this published 5 000 urban household data has its own value and has been used for trend analysis in some studies (e. g. Li, 2013), I found this sample shows some characteristics which do not reflect consistent trend with the former three waves of the survey, and are also different from the 10 000 urban household data collected in 2007. One of those characteristics is population age structure. This conclusion is based on the comparison between the summary statistics of the CHIPS 2007 urban 10 000 household data provided by Luo et al. (2007) and my own calculation using the CHIPS 2007 urban 5 000 household data. Therefore, it should be noted that the limitations of the data might influence the decomposition results between 2002 and 2007.

Chapter 3
Social Norms and Female Labor Force Participation in China

This chapter investigates the impact of social norms on married women's labor supply decision in China. Using data from the China General Social Survey (CGSS) and the China Family Panel Studies (CFPS), we find a strong and robust positive correlation between the labor supply behavior of a married woman and the former work experience of her mother-in-law. Our estimation results indicate that being raised by a working mother influences both a man's attitude toward gender roles and his household productivity, and therefore married women whose mothers-in-law were not working are themselves significantly less likely to participate in the labor force.

3.1 Introduction

Women's labor market attachment has declined dramatically in China Since the 1990s as the country makes its transition from a centrally-planned to a market-oriented economy. In the 1980s women had high labor force participation rates of more than 90 percent, and almost half of the labor force was female. Whereas in more recent years women are increasingly more likely to exit the formal labor market, and their participation rates are now less than 80 percent (Feng, Hu and Moffitt, 2015). This labor market trend in China reverses the pattern of

Chapter 3
Social Norms and Female Labor Force Participation in China

increasing female labor force participation experienced in the U. S. and other major developed economies in the past several decades. The explanations for the rising female labor force participation in the U. S. include the increase in women's real wage and education (Eckstein and Lifshitz, 2011), the technological advances in consumer durables (Greenwood, Seshadri and Yorukoglu, 2005) and the expansion of the service sector (Goldin, 1990; Lee and Wolpin, 2006).[①] Similar socioeconomic changes have also taken place in China Since the 1990s, yet there has been a continuous decline in women's involvement in the formal labor market. Recent studies to explain the puzzling decline of female labor supply in China have focused on factors such as the changing family structure (Maurer-Fazio et al., 2009; Shen, Zhang and Yan, 2012), the changing child care system after the economic reform (Du and Dong, 2010), and the rising housing price (Fu, Liao, and Zhang, 2016). This chapter suggests a new and complementary hypothesis and seeks to understand the role of preference formation and social norms on female labor supply behavior during a period of rapid socioeconomic transformation in China.

We follow the seminal work by Fernández, Fogli and Olivetti (2004) and argue that changes in social norms, in particular, men's gender role preferences and their household productivity, can be a significant factor in the continuing decrease in female labor market participation over time. The social norms examined in this paper are based on the observation that an increasing number of Chinese men, over time Since the 1990s, grew up in families where their mothers did not work. Growing up with a non-working mother can make a man more averse to having a working wife as his idea of gender roles and what the division of labor in the household may differ from the man with a working mother. The growing presence of this type of man in turn will make investing in market skills and becoming a working woman less attractive for women in the following generation. Alternatively, men may have similar preferences, but men brought up by non-working mothers may

---

[①] The literature on married women's labor supply is voluminous and cannot be fully reviewed here. Blundell and MaCurdy (1999) provided an excellent survey.

have lower household productivity arising perhaps from lower willingness to participate in housework. As the number of working mothers decreases in China, the proportion of men raised with non-working mothers increases, which may lead to a decrease in the number of working women of the next generation.

This chapter makes two important contributions to the existing literature. First, we are among the first to examine the impact of social norms on female labor supply in a fast-growing transition economy, which has witnessed drastic socioeconomic changes since the 1980s. Fernández, Fogli and Olivetti (2004) show that the wives of men whose mothers worked are themselves significantly more likely to work in the U. S. , and they argue that the growing number of men brought up in a family with a working mother has been a significant factor in the increasing female labor force participation. Several studies, including Kawaguchi and Miyazaki (2009) and Bütikofer (2013), have tested similar hypothesis by employing data from other countries. While Bütikofer (2013) found significant results for the intergenerational link between mother-in-law's working status and female labor supply in Switzerland, the results are not statistically significant in Japan according to Kawaguchi and Miyazaki (2009). All previous research is limited to mature economies sharing similar institutional settings and experiencing similar patterns of increased presence of women in the labor market. The purpose of this chapter is to investigate whether the work status of a married man's mother affects his wife's labor supply in China, a country with a very different economic and institutional environment and experiencing large decline in female labor force participation. This distinction is important because there is growing evidence that living under a specific political system or institution leads to adaptation of certain attitudes, beliefs and preferences. ① We examine whether the formation of one

---

① For example, Bowles (1998) emphasizes the role of economic institutions in the evolution of preferences and culture. Alesina and Fuchs-Schündeln (2007) show that the difference in preferences between former East and West Germans is due in large part to the direct effect of Communism. Giuliano and Spilimbergo (2014) find that the experience of macroeconomic shocks when young has long-lasting effects on beliefs and preferences. Alesina and Giuliano (2015) provide an extensive survey on the relationship between culture and institution.

particular set of attitudes and preferences, those towards married women's labor market participation, differs under the unique economic and institutional setting of China.

Second, our analysis moves beyond providing evidence that mother-in-law's working status matters for female labor force participation and quantifying the impact; the paper explores empirically two mechanisms through which mother-in-law's employment status and married women's employment status are linked. The first mechanism emphasizes that men grown up with non-working mothers tend to be more averse to having working wives than other men (preference channel), and the second mechanism explores the possibility that men grown up with non-working mothers tend to be less productive or less willing to participate in housework (household productivity channel). Fernández, Fogli and Olivetti (2004) presented a dynamic framework to show that both channels give rise to similar intergenerational link between mothers-in-law and women of next generation, but they did not provide any empirical evidence on these underlying mechanisms. In this paper, we directly test and distinguish these two assumptions by examining the effect of being raised by a working mother on men's stated preferences regarding gender role attitudes and the effect of the work status of mothers-in-law on married women's time spent on household chores.

To estimate the effect of mothers-in-law's working status on married women's labor force participation, we use microdata from the China General Social Survey (CGSS) and the China Family Panel Studies (CFPS). We show that the employment status of a married woman is positively and significantly correlated with whether her mother-in-law worked, even after controlling for many other background characteristics that may be driving the positive relationship. We find that having a working mother-in-law increases the probability that a married women works by 6 to 16 percentage points depending on the specification and the data set used. The estimation results provide strong evidence that social norms do influence the labor supply behavior of married women in China. Although China has a different economic and institutional environment compared to the U.S., we find a similar intergenerational link as in Fernández, Fogli and Olivetti (2004) that wives of men with working mothers are more likely to participate in the labor market.

Furthermore, we obtain empirical evidence on the underlying mechanisms driving the observed intergeneration correlation. The CGSS directly asks respondents about their attitudes toward women's labor market participation and their subjective well-being. To test the validity of the preference channel, we analyze whether mother's work status affects her son's response to the gender role questions. We also examine whether the effect of a wife's contribution to household income on her husband's satisfaction depends on the work experience of his mother. We find that men raised by non-working mothers are more likely to agree with traditional gender stereotype and that a wife's contribution to household income increases her husband's satisfaction less if he was raised by a non-working mother. The CFPS contains a time use module, which includes questions about respondent's time spent on various activities. To test the household productivity channel, we examine whether a married woman's time spent on household chores depends on the former work experience of her mother-in-law. We find that married women whose mothers-in-law were not working on average spend 16 percent more time during weekdays and 12 percent more time overall on housework chores compared to otherwise similar women whose mothers-in-law worked. These results are likely driven by the fact that men grown up with non-working mothers tend to be less productive or less willing to participate in or outsource housework. Taken together, the evidence indicates that mother's work status affects social norms in terms of men's gender role preferences and their household productivity, and in turn, affects the labor force participation rate of married women in the next generation.

The study in this chapter is closely related to a growing literature that emphasizes the long-run impact of changing social norms. Besides Fernández, Fogli and Olivetti (2004), Goldin (1991) argues that the attitudes toward working women changed considerably during World War II as a large number of women

Chapter 3
Social Norms and Female Labor Force Participation in China

entered the labor market. Fortin (2005) finds that egalitarian views toward gender role and work values are positively associated with female employment rates across 25 OECD countries. Fernández and Fogli (2009) and Fernández (2013) investigate the role of culture in explaining changes in female employment. [①] Our findings provide new evidence on the effects of social norms on female labor supply in China. The employment status of a man's mother can shape his gender-role preference and practice, and as a result influence women's employment choice. This kind of intergenerational propagation mechanism may be quite robust across different economic and institutional settings. While most papers on social norms examine the impact of social norms on human behavior (e.g., female labor supply), this paper also focuses on the channels through which social norms evolve over time. [②]

The rest of the chapter is organized as follows. Section 3.2 provides an overview of the changes in social and gender identity norms in China. Section 3.3 briefly reviews the literature. Section 3.4 describes our sample and introduces our empirical framework. Estimation results are reported in Section 3.5, and Section 3.6 checks their robustness. Section 3.7 concludes.

3.2 Social and Gender Identity Norms in China

Social and gender identity norms about what is appropriate for men to do and what is appropriate for women to do vary both across societies and over time. China experienced tremendous changes in prevalent gender role attitudes over its history, and likewise, equally drastic changes in women's labor market choices and

---

[①] A few other papers linking social norms to female labor supply include Reimers (1985), Charles, Guryan and Pan (2009) and Farré and Vella (2013). See Bertrand (2011) for an extensive survey on the relationship between social and gender identity norms and women's labor market choices and outcomes.

[②] The paper by Alesina, Giuliano and Nunn (2013), which analyzes the origin of one kind of social norms gender roles, is one of the few exceptions.

outcomes.

The traditional Chinese family and society were extremely patriarchal and patrilineal. Women were put at a disadvantaged position relative to men, and their primary roles were defined as wives and mothers. From the Han dynasty onward in imperial China, Confucianism largely defined the mainstream discourse on gender. A set of basic moral principles, were established specifically for women. According to these principles, a virtuous woman is supposed to follow the lead of the males in her family. Women were denied the opportunity for education, and their activities were confined to the domestic arena. While women may engage in some income-generating activities, such as domestic sidelines, they could do so only with the permission of the men (Zhang, 2019). The long history of imperial endorsement of Confucianism had reinforced this obligatory gender roles and the notion of women's inferiority during the pre-modern time in China.

Since the collapse of the Qing Dynasty in 1911, gender-role attitudes and women's socioeconomic status had undergone remarkable changes. The New Culture Movement of the mid 1910s and 1920s revolted against Confucianism, called for an end to the patriarchal family, and advocated individual freedom and women's liberation. As a result, some women began to acquire formal education and work outside home in order to fight for their economic independence.

After the founding of the People's Republic of China in 1949, the National Marriage Law was enacted and promulgated in 1950, which legalized the free-choice of marriage and equalized the rights of husbands and wives in the family. It also explicitly granted wives the freedom to participate in the labor market. Since the 1950s, enormous progress has been made in increasing women's employment opportunities and their education level. With guaranteed employment under the state-controlled economy, female labor force participation was almost universal. For instance, in 1988, the labor force participation rate was 93% for women between the prime ages of 16 and 55 (Ge and Yang, 2014). At the same time, women's educational attainment also improved tremendously and caught up with that of men over the years (Wu and Zhang, 2010). As women's socioeconomic status was greatly elevated, there were radical departures from traditional gender-role views. Egalitarian gender role attitudes, such as women being able to hold half of the sky, were accepted by more people as the norm.

Despite the substantial improvements, it should be noted that some of the traditional notions and practices concerning gender relations and the family have persisted. With respect to domestic arena, women are still mainly responsible for caring for children and the household, and they are also responsible for the major share of housework (Xie, 2013). With respect to public arena, severe occupation segregation is common. Women's political participation is still very low, and women are underrepresented in higher-level administrative or managerial positions. After the inception of economic reform, female labor force participation rate started to decline in the 1980s, along with a widening gender gap in earnings (Ge and Yang, 2014). The decrease in female labor participation accelerated in the late 1990s during the state-sector restructuring, and female labor force participation rate dropped to less than 80 percent in recent years (Feng, Hu and Moffitt, 2015). As China shifted from command labor arrangement under planning, which emphasized gender equality, to a system of market determination of employment and pay, the traditional views and practices regarding gender relations and division of labor within the family have somewhat rebounded.

Although contemporary China has witnessed tremendous improvements in women's socioeconomic status and has moved towards a more egalitarian society, there are still continuations of traditional social and gender identity norms. Therefore, it is of great empirical importance to investigate whether and how much such evolving social norms can affect women's labor supply behavior.

3.3 Literature Review

There is a growing body of literature investigating the relationship between social attitudes and female labor force participation. Efforts have been made both theoretically and empirically. For instance, Fernández (2013) established a theoretical model in which female labor force participation and culture are co-determined. Empirically, Fortin (2009) studied the relationship between women's work decisions and their own gender-role attitudes, while Charles et al. (2009) explored the relationship between female labor market participation and men's views on gender role questions. [①] Based on these findings, a natural question to ask is what drives gender identity. Several factors have been investigated as potential driving forces, such as the innovations in contraception (Goldin and Katz, 2000), the AIDS crisis (Fortin, 2009), early childhood experience (Fernández et al., 2004), and one's cultural background (Fernández and Fogli, 2009), as well as the historical origins of the current differences in gender roles across societies, such as traditional agricultural practices (Alesina et al., 2011). Furthermore, another natural question followed is whether there exists any relationship between the driving forces of gender identity and female labor force participation decision (Fernández et al., 2004; Farré and Vella, 2007; Olivetti et al., 2013; Alesina et al., 2011), and if so, the existence of other underlying mechanisms for such relationship besides the mechanism through social norms.

The findings of Fernández et al. (2004) contribute to the last realm of inquiry. In their paper, the relationship between female labor force participation and one of the potential driving forces of men's gender role preference, early childhood experience, has been investigated, and another potential underlying mechanism has been proposed. Specifically, in their seminal paper, Fernández et al. (2004) first provide evidence for the intergenerational link between the working behavior of a woman and her mother-in-law, that is, men who were raised by working mothers are more likely to have working wives, as suggested by the strong cross-sectional regression results. This relationship is significant and robust to the inclusion of vari-

---

[①] There is abundant literature on the relationship between gender-role attitudes and labor market outcomes. Please refer to Vella (1994), Fortin (2005), Fernández and Fogli (2009), and Farré and Vella (2007) for more instances.

ous background characteristics of the couple. To further establish causality, they use the variation in mobilization rate across different states in the U. S. during World War II and examine the dynamic implications of this event. Additionally, they propose the potential mechanisms underlying this positive correlation are working through the influence of working mothers on their sons. Particularly, they argue that men grown up with working mothers tend to be less averse to having a working wife than other men (preference channel), and they are also more productive at housework (household productivity channel). Those two features would allow their wives to spend more time in the labor market. However, they did not present empirical evidence to support these underlying mechanisms.

Complementary to Fernández et al. (2004), Morrill and Morrill (2013) provide an alternative and non-causal explanation for this statistical relationship found in Fernández et al. (2004). They claim it is possible that the causal relationship actually lies between mothers and daughters, and the relationship between the working behavior of the women and their mothers-in-law could simply result from assortative mating. Specifically, it can be the case that daughters with working mothers are first influenced by their mothers, form their preferences regarding labor market participation, and then select appropriate spouses who were also raised by working mothers. In short, Morrill and Morrill (2013) focused on the intergeneration preference formation from mothers to daughters, while Fernández et al. (2004) focused on the intergeneration link from mothers to sons. To support this alternative explanation, Morrill and Morrill (2013) tested the relationship between the labor supply choices of mothers and daughters using the same data with Fernández et al. (2004) and found women are more likely to participate in the labor force if their mothers worked.

Inspired by Fernández et al. (2004)'s innovative paper, several authors tested this "mothers and sons" story using the datasets from different countries, and further explored the underlying mechanisms and other implications of the paper. Kawaguchi and Miyazaki (2009) replicated Fernández et al. (2004) using the Japanese General Social Surveys (JGSS) data, yet their results are not statistically significant. In addition, they investigated the relationship between mothers' working status and their sons' gender-role attitudes, and they found men raised by full-time working mothers are more likely to develop the preference favorable towards working women. Their study supplements Fernández et al. (2004) by directly testing one of the underlying mechanisms. In another application, Bütikofer (2013) replicated Fernández et al. (2004)'s cross-section analysis using the Swiss Household Panel 2005 and gained significant results. As Kawaguchi and Miyazaki (2009), Bütikofer (2013) also tested the preference channel, but used a different approach. Particularly, instead of directly examining the relationship between husband's stated gender role preference and the former labor market status of his mother, Bütikofer (2013) tested the systematic difference in utility function among the two types of men using a satisfaction estimation. The results show that the effect of the wife's labor market integration on her husband's well-being diverges depending on the former employment status of his mother. In particular, the wife's contribution to household income affects her husband's degree of satisfaction negatively if her husband was raised by a non-working mother, while has no significant impact on her husband's wellbeing if her husband was raised by a working mother.

3.4 Empirical Analysis

3.4.1 Data

The main data sets used in this chapter is the 2010 wave of China General Social Survey (CGSS).① The 2010 CGSS adopts a multi-stage stratified sam-

---

① The CGSS is also known as the China GSS. General Social Survey (GSS) has been conducted by the National Opinion Research Center (NORC) at the University of Chicago on American society since 1972. The GSS is the main dataset used in Fernández, Fogli and Olivetti (2004) for cross-sectional analysis.

pling design. It covers all 31 provincial units in mainland China and 11 754 households. The CGSS contains rich information on each respondent's employment status, demographic characteristics, and social attitudes, as well as their spouses' characteristics. For the purpose of our study, the key variable of interest is "what was your mother's employment status when you were at the age of 14". The respondent's mother is defined as employed if she was an employee, a farmer, or self-employed. In the data, we can simultaneously observe a married man's mother's previous employment status and his wife's current working status. A woman is defined as a labor market participant if she engages in any type of job for the purpose of earning economic income in the last week, or not engages in such kind of job but actively seeking for jobs in the last 3 months.

We supplement the analysis with a data set called the China Family Panel Studies (CFPS). The CFPS is a nationally representative longitudinal survey of Chinese communities, families and individuals. The baseline CFPS survey was launched in 2010 covering 14 960 households and 42 590 individuals, and the first follow-up survey was carried out in 2012. The CFPS sample covers 25 provincial units, representing 95% of the Chinese population. Like the CGSS, the CFPS survey also contains rich information on employment and demographics. In the CFPS, a woman is defined as a non-participant if she is not working because she does not want to work, loses working capacity due to age, disability or illness, or is retired, attending schooling or doing housework. In the 2012 follow-up survey, retrospective information on the employment status of each respondent's mother was asked. [1] One limitation of the CFPS is that it does not include some of the husband's background variables, such as his religion and the wealth of his family of origin. Without these variables, it would be difficult to distinguish the proposed hypothesis from several competing explanations. Therefore, we use the results gained from the CFPS as a robust check to the benchmark results obtained

---

[1] The key question of interest is "what was your mother's occupation when you were at the age of 14". If the occupation code of the respondent's mother is neither "not applicable" nor "unemployed", the respondent's mother is defined as employed.

from the CGSS.

We restrict our samples to be the married women aged 30 to 50 with urban registration (*hukou*).① In addition, since our study focuses on the labor supply behavior of the female urban workers (employees), the wives who are employers or self-employed are excluded. The summary statistics for both samples are presented in Table 3.1.

Table 3.1　　Descriptive Statistics: CGSS and CPFS Data

	CGSS		CFPS	
	Mean	S.D.	Mean	S.D.
Wife participated	0.71	0.46	0.80	0.40
Mother-in-law worked	0.75	0.43	0.74	0.44
Husband's age	42.56	6.40	42.30	6.73
Husband's education (%)				
Middle school and below	28.98		39.74	
High school and tech	58.64		46.54	
University and above	12.38		13.71	
Husband's income	10.12	0.92	10.16	0.98
Wife's age	40.26	5.69	40.46	6.04
Wife's education (%)				
Middle school and below	38.23		43.74	
High school and tech	52.65		44.92	
University and above	9.12		11.34	
Number of children under 18	1.21	0.54	1.18	0.52
Husband's father's education (%)				
Middle school and below	81.36		79.81	
High school and tech	15.51		16.85	
University and above	3.13		3.35	

---

① The current household registration status for the wife is non-agricultural, or *lanyin*, or *jumin*.

continued

	CGSS		CFPS	
	Mean	S. D.	Mean	S. D.
Husband's mother's education (%)				
Middle school and below	88.44		90.82	
High school and tech	10.61		8.21	
University and above	0.95		0.97	
Number of observations	735		926	

Note: The CGSS sample is restricted to be the married women aged 30 to 50 with urban registration (*hukou*) who are neither employers nor self-employed. The CFPS sample consists of the married women aged 30 to 50 with urban registration who are not engaged in self-employed business.

3.4.2 The Empirical Model

Our empirical specification follows the framework first proposed by Fernández, Fogli and Olivetti (2004), with several adjustments in view of the objective of our paper. In particular, in order to study the relationship between the working behavior of a man's mother and that of his wife, the following model is estimated:

$$P_i^w = \beta_0 + X_i'\beta_1 + \beta_2 E_i^m + \epsilon_i \qquad (3.1)$$

where the dependent variable P_i^w is the participation indicator of the wife, E_i^m represents the employment status of the wife's mother-in-law during adolescence of her husband, and X_i is a vector of background variables to control for alternative hypothesis, which differs in different specifications. E_i^m is our key variable of interest. The main purpose of this empirical model is to rule out other characteristics of the couple as the main determinants of the intergeneration correlation between the wife's and the mother-in-law's employment status, thus various control variables are added sequentially.

More specifically, seven specifications have been considered. [1] The base-

---

[1] Specifications examined are similar for both data sources. Since the CGSS contains more comprehensive information on the background of the couple and is used as the dataset to gain the baseline results, the specifications discussed here are the ones used for the CGSS.

line model (i) controls for several characteristics of the husband which may influence the working behavior of his wife, such as his age, his education attainment and his income level. Model (ii) controls for the age and education level of the wife. In model (iii), we include the characteristics of both the husband and the wife, and in model (iv) we also add the number of children. In model (v), in addition to the husband's characteristics contained in model (i), we also add a number of variables concerning other background characteristics of the husband: the education attainment of his parents, his own religion, and his self-assessed ranking of his family in the society when he was fourteen.① Model (vi) modifies model (v) by including the wife's characteristics. The final specification completes model (vi) by controlling the number of children. In each model, we also include the provincial dummies.

The controls are added sequentially to account for alternative explanations and to take care of the endogenous concern, since this positive correlation between the working behavior of a woman and her mother-in-law could be driven by some observed background characteristics of the couple, such as religion and family wealth, so we need to control for those factors in order to rule out the possibility that those background characteristics are in fact the main drivers of the observed intergeneration correlation. For instance, one could argue the observed positive correlation in working behavior is primarily driven by assortative matching in religion: a man raised by a working mother from a religion encouraging women to work may also marry a woman from the same religion. To control for this possibility, we need to include the husband's religion in our model. Another potential explanation concerns family wealth: it is possible that a man's mother worked while he was young because of low family wealth; since a man coming from a low-wealth family is more likely to have low family wealth himself, his wife would also be more likely to work. In this case, the observed positive correlation in

---

① Fernández, Fogli and Olivetti (2004) used the religion in which the husband was raised as an control variable, but we use the husband's religion instead, since 2/3 of the former definition are missing values and using it would greatly shrink our sample size.

work choice may simply reflect the relationship between family wealth and the labor supply behavior of a married woman.

3.5 Estimation Results

In this section, we present the baseline cross-sectional evidence obtained from the empirical model. Consistent with our hypothesis, we find a strong and robust positive relationship between the labor force participation of the wife and the working behavior of her mother-in-law when her husband was at the age 14 in China. Specifically, cross-sectional evidence suggests the wives of the husbands brought up by working mothers are more likely to participate in the labor market. This relationship remains robust to the inclusion of various control variables. In addition, we test two potential underlying mechanisms and present empirical evidence for both.

3.5.1 Cross-Sectional Evidence

We first estimate a series of specifications presented by equation (3.1) using the 2010 sample of the CGSS. Table 3.2 exhibits the estimation results for all seven specifications. We run both the Linear Probability model (LPM) and the Probit model using robust standard errors. The results gained from both approaches are similar in significance level and magnitude, and we report here the results of the Linear Probability model. The estimated correlation between the working behavior of the wife and her mother-in-law is positive, large in magnitude and statistically significant. The results remains robust in all seven specifications. In particular, the LPM estimation of the baseline model shows that having a husband who was raised by a working mother increases the married woman's probability of participating in the labor market by 16.2 percentage points, and this effect is significant at 0.1 percent level. Even after controlled for all the background variables which could potentially drive this positive correlation [model (vii)], this effect is still large in magnitude (13.2 percentage points) and significant at 0.1 percent level.

Table 3.2   Cross-Sectional Evidence (CGSS): Linear Probability Regression of Married Woman's Participation Status on Her Mother-in-law's Work Status

	(i)	(ii)	(iii)	(iv)	(v)	(vi)	(vii)
Mother-in-law worked	0.1618 *** (0.0432)	0.1284 *** (0.0394)	0.1512 *** (0.0425)	0.1441 *** (0.0433)	0.1512 *** (0.0455)	0.1390 *** (0.0447)	0.1318 *** (0.0456)
Husband's age	-0.0107 *** (0.0026)		-0.0081 (0.0050)	-0.0071 (0.0050)	-0.0093 *** (0.0027)	-0.0066 (0.0052)	-0.0066 (0.0053)
Husband's income	-0.0176 (0.0225)		-0.0389 * (0.0228)	-0.0398 * (0.0225)	-0.0268 (0.0231)	-0.0460 * (0.0235)	-0.0479 ** (0.0232)
Wife's age		-0.0084 *** (0.0026)	-0.0012 (0.0056)	-0.0013 (0.0056)		-0.0018 (0.0058)	-0.0007 (0.0060)
Children				-0.0813 ** (0.0367)			-0.0887 ** (0.0383)
Husband's education	yes		yes	yes	yes	yes	yes
Wife's education		yes	yes	yes		yes	yes
Husband's parents' education					yes	yes	yes
Religion					yes	yes	yes
Income 14					yes	yes	yes
Region	yes	yes	yes	yes	yes	yes	yes
Observations	757	882	757	750	736	736	729
Adjusted R-squared	0.108	0.122	0.152	0.157	0.112	0.150	0.155

Note: Robust standard errors are reported in parentheses. The dependent variable is the participation indicator of the wife. Mother-in-law worked variable represents the husband's mother's employment status when he was at the age 14. Religion is a set of dummies for the husband's religion. Income 14 is a set of dummies for the husband's self-assessed ranking of his family in the society when he was fourteen. Region are the provincial dummies. A constant term is included in all the specifications.

* significant at 10%, ** significant at 5%, *** significant at 1%.

Compared with the results in Fernández, Fogli and Olivetti (2004), this estimated effect is smaller in magnitude, but stronger in significance level. Besides the cultural difference between the U. S. and China, several reasons may account for the difference. First, the time periods being investigated are different. Fernández, Fogli and Olivetti (2004) used the GSS in the years 1988 and 1994, whereas we used the CGSS in 2010. Second, we use married women's participation status as the dependent variable whereas Fernández, Fogli and Olivetti (2004) focused on employment status. They had information on whether the man's mother worked for as long as a year after her son was born and before he was 14, but we only have information on whether a man's mother worked when he was 14 years old.

Although the cross-sectional results using the CGSS provide strong evidence that wives with working mothers-in-law are more likely to participate in the labor market and this relationship remains robust to the inclusion of various control variables, we use the 2012 sample of the CFPS as an alternative data source. We estimate the similar specifications with various controls using the CFPS. Table 3.3 reports the estimation results. Models (i) – (iv) contain the same set of control variables as before. Overall, the results are smaller in magnitude and less significant. However, in all the specifications, the estimated correlation between the working behavior of the women and their mothers-in-law are still significant at 10 percent level. Starting from the model (v), the specifications are slightly different from the previous analysis due to the lack of certain background variables of the husband. Specifically, since the CFPS does not have the information concerning the husband's own religion and his self-assessment of his family in the society when he was fourteen, these two variables are not included in models (v) – (vii), but all the other variables in the CGSS specifications are also incorporated in the CFPS specifications. As the previous analysis, the estimated correlation between the working behavior of the wife and her mother-in-law is positive, large in magnitude, and at least statistically significant at 10 percent level. In sum, the results remain relatively robust across different datasets.

Table 3.3   Cross-Sectional Evidence (CFPS): Linear Probability Regression of Married Woman's Participation Status on Her Mother-in-law's Work Status

	(i)	(ii)	(iii)	(iv)	(v)	(vi)	(vii)
Mother-in-law worked	0.0723 ** (0.0337)	0.0634 ** (0.0277)	0.0636 * (0.0334)	0.0634 * (0.0333)	0.0761 ** (0.0350)	0.0660 * (0.0345)	0.0662 * (0.0344)
Husband's age	−0.0055 ** (0.0022)		−0.0077 * (0.0045)	−0.0077 * (0.0045)	−0.0048 ** (0.0024)	−0.0075 (0.0047)	−0.0075 (0.0047)
Husband's income	−0.0057 (0.0154)		−0.0111 (0.0153)	−0.0104 (0.0153)	−0.0076 (0.0157)	−0.0135 (0.0157)	−0.0132 (0.0156)
Wife's age		−0.0017 (0.0020)	0.0052 (0.0049)	0.0057 (0.0049)		0.0056 (0.0050)	0.0060 (0.0050)
Children				−0.0482 (0.0316)			−0.0392 (0.0320)
Husband's education	yes		yes	yes	yes	yes	yes
Wife's education		yes	yes	yes		yes	yes
Husband's parents' education					yes	yes	yes
Region	yes	yes	yes	yes	yes	yes	yes
Observations	954	1 333	954	954	924	924	924
Adjusted R-squared	0.040	0.067	0.061	0.063	0.041	0.064	0.065

Note: Robust standard errors are reported in parentheses. The dependent variable is the participation indicator of the wife. Mother-in-law worked variable represents the husband's mother's employment status when he was at the age 14. Region are the provincial dummies. A constant term is included in all the specifications.

* significant at 10%, ** significant at 5%, *** significant at 1%.

One special feature of the CFPS is that it has personal identifiers for each household member and as a result we can link the husband and wife for each married couple. Therefore the data contains detailed background information on both the husband and the wife. In particular, we can control for the former employment status of the wife's own mother as well as the education level of the wife's parents. Therefore, we augment model (ii) by including the above three variables. After the employment status of the wife's own mother and her parents' education dummies are included in the model, the estimated effect of whether a man's mother worked on whether his wife participates is still significant at 5 percent level, while the estimated effect of her own mother is insignificant, meaning growing up with a working mother does not influence the daughter's labor force participation decision. This finding is consistent with the findings in Fernández, Fogli and Olivetti (2004). Likewise, we augment model (vii) by adding the aforementioned variables concerning the wife's parents. Although the results in this specification are not significant for both her mother-in-law and her own mother, the p-value of her mother-in-law variable is still close to 10 percent. Taken together, these results can serve as evidence to rule out the possibility that this positive correlation is primarily driven by assortative mating.

3.5.2 Testing for Potential Underlying Mechanisms

In this part, we present empirical evidence that the positive correlation between the working behavior of the wife and her mother-in-law is mainly driven through the working mother-in-law's influence on her son. We mainly consider two potential channels. First of all, it is possible that men with working mothers are less averse towards having a working wife than the men who grew up with non-working mothers. Therefore, the difference in the husband's preference could serve as one underlying mechanism for this positive correlation. Alternatively, even if the husbands have similar preferences, men with working mothers may be more productive in housework than other men, which might also affect the probability that their wives participate and serve as another mechanism for this positive association. [①] Fernández, Fogli and Olivetti (2004) proposed the above two potential channels in a theoretical framework, but did not provide empirical tests for them. In this section, we directly test these two potential underlying mecha-

---

① It should be noted that this difference in household productivity might result from men's different attitudes toward housework.

nisms. We find that the positive correlation between the working behavior of the wife and her mother-in-law is primarily driven by the fact that her working mother-in-law has influenced both her husband's gender role preference and productivities in home production.

1. Preference Channel

Men raised by working mothers may be less averse to a working wife than men who grew up in the traditional families. In particular, this difference in their utility functions could be directly reflected in their stated gender role preferences, or be inferred from their self-assessed happiness level.

One hypothesis is that men raised by working mothers should have more egalitarian gender role preferences. The CGSS 2010 has several attitudinal questions regarding the respondent's gender role preferences, which allows us to test this hypothesis directly. Specifically, in CGSS 2010 the respondents were asked whether they "totally disagree", "somewhat disagree", "neutral", "somewhat agree" or "totally agree" with each of the following two statements: "Men should focus on career, while women should focus on family" and "During a recession, female workers should be dismissed first".

Both the OLS and the Probit regression are used to test this hypothesis. The dependent variable is the male respondent's response to each statement. We recode the response into a binary variable by combining "totally disagree" and "somewhat disagree" as "0" representing the egalitarian gender role preference, and combining "neutral" "somewhat agree" and "totally agree" as "1" representing the traditional gender role attitude. The explanatory variables include the mother's employment status while the man was fourteen, and other husband's background characteristics. To be specific, we control for the husband's age and education level, the provincial dummies, the education attainment of his parents, his religion, and his self-assessed ranking of his family in the society when he was 14 years old. We include the husband's background variables in order to control for other potential explanations for the formation of his gender role preference. Additionally, adding these background variables also helps to estimate the parameter consistently, since those variables may affect both a man's gender role preference and the working status of his mother during his adolescence.

Table 3.4 reports the regression results, which are consistent with our hypothesis. Particularly, men brought up by working mothers are approximately 8% less likely to agree with the statement "Men should focus on work, while women should focus on family" than men raised by non-working mothers. This difference is statistically significant at 5 percent level. For the second statement, "During a recession, female workers should be dismissed first", men with working mothers are approximately 7% less likely to agree than the traditional type of men, and the estimates are significant at 10 percent level.

Table 3.4　Preference Channel: Husband's Stated Gender Role Preferences

Statement	"Men should focus on career, while women should focus on family."		"During a recession, female workers should be dismissed first."	
	OLS	Probit	OLS	Probit
Mother-in-law worked	-0.0780 ** (0.0389)	-0.0817 ** (0.0390)	-0.0716 * (0.0388)	-0.0690 * (0.0363)
Husband's age	0.0012 (0.0025)	0.0010 (0.0025)	0.0016 (0.0025)	0.0015 (0.0024)
Husband's education	yes	yes	yes	yes
Husband's parents' education	yes	yes	yes	yes
Religion	yes	yes	yes	yes
Income 14	yes	yes	yes	yes
Region	yes	yes	yes	yes
Observations	856	843	854	852

Note: Robust standard errors are reported in parentheses. For the Probit model, marginal effects are calculated and reported. The dependent variable is the male respondent's response to each statement, which is a binary variable equals one if the respondent agrees. Mother-in-law worked variable represents the husband's mother's employment status when he was at the age 14. Religion is a set of dummies for the husband's religion. Income 14 is a set of dummies for the husband's self-assessed ranking of his family in the society when he was fourteen. Region are the provincial dummies. A constant term is included in all the specifications.

* significant at 10%, ** significant at 5%, *** significant at 1%.

Preference channel also implies that men who grew up with working mothers may have different utility functions from those raised up by non-working mothers. To account for this difference, Fernández, Fogli and Olivetti (2004) introduce a new term in married men's utility function. This new term measures the direct disutility from his wife's market time. To test this proposed difference in their utility functions, Bütikofer (2013) examines the relationship between wife's contribution to household income and her husband's satisfaction level. His results suggest that the effect of a wife's labor market integration on her husband's well-being significantly differs for the two types of men.

Based on Bütikofer (2013), we use a question asked in the CGSS 2010 regarding the respondent's subjective well-being to further examine the preference mechanism. The question is "In general, do you think your life is happy?" The choices are "very unhappy", "somewhat unhappy", "in some in-between state", "somewhat happy" and "very happy". We recode the responses into a dummy variable, which equals one if the response is "somewhat happy" or "very happy", and equals zero otherwise. This dummy variable serves as the dependent variable. In particular, we estimate both the LPM and the Probit models based on the following specification:

$$H_i^h = \beta_0 + X_i'\beta_1 + \beta_2 C_i^w + \beta_3 T_i^h + \beta_4 C_i^w \times T_i^h + \epsilon_i \quad (3.2)$$

The key explanatory variable concerning the wife's labor market integration is measured by her contribution to the household income (C_i^w). Specifically, the wife's income contribution equals her annual income divided by the annual household income of her family. Additionally, to distinguish the two types of men, we define an indicator variable (T_i^h), which equals one for men who grew up with non-working mothers, and equals zero for men raised by working mothers. Lastly, we generate an interaction term of the wife's contribution to the household income and the indicator variable representing the traditional type of men ($C_i^w \times T_i^h$). This interaction term is constructed to examine whether there exists a difference in the effect of wife's income contribution on husband's subjective well-being depending on his mother's former working status. Besides the wife's income contribution, the traditional type indicator and the interaction term, other explanatory variables include wife's and husband's age, education attainment of the couple, logarithm of the husband's annual personal income, logarithm of the household income, number of children, the husband's religion, the husband's parents' education level, and provincial dummies.

The hypothesis is that wife's labor market integration should have an additional negative effect on the subjective well-being of the traditional type of man compared to the non-traditional type. Since we are interested in providing evidence for the existence of this difference, the main focus is the estimates of the interaction term. The results of the Probit model are consistent with our hypothesis, which are presented in Table 3.5. The estimated coefficient of the interaction term is negative and significant at 10% level, which supports the existence of the difference in the utility function for the two types of men. Specifically, it means that wife's income contribution exerts an additional negative impact on the husband's degree of happiness for the traditional type of men, and this negative effect is statistically significant. Therefore, the results could be taken as a evidence for the systematic difference in the utility function of the two types of men.

Table 3.5 Preference Channel: The Husband's Subjective Well-being

	LPM	Probit
Wife's income contribution (i)	0.3581 *** (0.1333)	0.2999 *** (0.1035)
Mother not in labor force (ii)	0.0920 (0.0651)	0.0988 (0.0623)
Interaction term (i × ii)	−0.2838 (0.1752)	−0.2844 * (0.1604)
Husband's age	0.0097 (0.0061)	0.0089 * (0.0053)
Wife's age	−0.0142 ** (0.0065)	−0.0140 ** (0.0058)

continued

	LPM	Probit
Husband's income	0.1803 *** (0.0609)	0.1564 *** (0.0472)
Household income	-0.0610 (0.0620)	-0.0268 (0.0489)
Children	0.0525 * (0.0317)	0.0460 (0.0291)
Education attainment of the couple	yes	yes
Husband's parents' education	yes	yes
Religion	yes	yes
Region	yes	yes
Observations	634	612

Note: Robust standard errors are reported in parentheses. For the Probit model, marginal effects are calculated and reported. The dependent variable is a binary variable which equals one if the husband feels happy. The wife's income contribution equals her annual income divided by the annual household income of her family. Mother not in labor force variable (the traditional type indicator) is an indicator variable which equals one for men who grew up with non-working mothers. Religion is a set of dummies for the husband's religion. Income 14 is a set of dummies for the husband's self-assessed ranking of his family in the society when he was fourteen. Region are the provincial dummies. A constant term is included in all the specifications.

* significant at 10%, ** significant at 5%, *** significant at 1%.

From the results in Table 3.5, it is also interesting to note that wife's contribution to the household income exerts a positive effect on the subjective well-being of the husband from both types, and this effect is statistically significant. This finding is different from Bütikofer (2013), whose results suggest that wife's income contribution has statistically insignificant effects on the husband's well-being. This divergence might provide evidence supporting the view that culture background and institutional setting can have long-lasting impact on individual beliefs (Alesina and Schündeln, 2005).

2. Endowment Channel

Mother-in-law could also influence the participation decision of her daughter-in-law via endowment channel. Specifically, men brought up by working mothers may be more productive in housework, or be more willing to engage in housework, or be more indifferent of outsourcing housework than the men with non-working mothers.① This difference in "endowments" among the two types of husbands could affect their wives' time spent on housework and thereby influence their labor market participation decisions.

The 2010 wave of the CFPS contains the Time Use Module which includes questions about the number of hours spent on various activities during the weekdays and the weekend, which allows us to investigate the potential endowment channel. The relationship of interest is the one between the female respondent's time spent on household chores and the former working experience of her mother-in-law. Therefore, based on the literature on household time allocation (Hwang, 2016), we estimate the following equation:

$$Y_i = \beta_0 + \beta_1 WorkMIL_i + X_i'\beta_2 + \epsilon_i \qquad (3.3)$$

where Y_i is the wife's time spent on household chores (overall or weekday). We did not use the husband's housework time as the dependent variable, since a working mother could influence her son's household productivity or attitudes towards housework and thereby her daughter-in-law's housework time through other channels as well, such as her son's inclination to outsourcing housework. The key variable of interest, the former working status of a woman's mother-in-law, is represented by $WorkMIL_i$.② X_i includes the working hours and income of the husband and the wife, their family income, the number of children under 18, the age and education level of the couple, the information on whether they are living with their parents, the occupation of the wife, her health status and the provincial dummies.

The same sample restrictions are imposed as in the CFPS 2012. Besides, we only keep the married couples with spouse present. Table 3.6 shows the results in

---

① In other words, they do not mind their wives doing less (Hwang, 2016).
② Since the CFPS 2010 does not include questions on the former working status of the respondent's parents, we use the information reported by the same individual in the CFPS 2012 instead.

which the coefficient on *WorkMIL* is significant in both models and large in magnitude. In particular, the estimates in model (1) indicate that women with working mothers-in-law spend 1.47 hours less on housework chores per week compared with women with non-working mothers-in-law, after the related demographic backgrounds and working status of the couple have been controlled; while model (2) suggests that women with working mothers-in-law spend 1.23 hours less on household chores per week during the weekdays. Since the average hours spent on housework chores of the sample used in regression are 12.34 hours per week and 7.72 hours during the weekdays, the effect of having a working mother-in-law on the woman's housework time is substantial.

Table 3.6 Household Productivity Channel: Wife's Time Spent on Housework

	(1)	(2)
	Housework Time	Housework Time (Weekday)
Mother-in-law worked	-1.4701 * (0.7969)	-1.2302 ** (0.5998)
Wife's working hours	-0.0877 ** (0.0339)	-0.0645 ** (0.0280)
Husband's working hours	0.0393 ** (0.0188)	0.0308 ** (0.0153)
Adjusted family income	-0.0000 (0.0000)	-0.0000 (0.0000)
Number of children under 18	0.9256 (0.8648)	0.2822 (0.6327)
Wife's age	0.3678 *** (0.1164)	0.2395 *** (0.0923)
Wife's income	-0.0001 *** (0.0000)	-0.0001 *** (0.0000)

continued

	(1)	(2)
	Housework Time	Housework Time (Weekday)
Husband's income	0.0000 ** (0.0000)	0.0000 * (0.0000)
Living arrangements	yes	yes
Husband's age and education	yes	yes
Wife's education, occupation and health status	yes	yes
Region	yes	yes
Observations	409	409
Adjusted R-squared	0.116	0.097

Note: Robust standard errors are reported in parentheses. Linear probablity model is used for both specifications. The dependent variable is the wife's time spent on household chores (overall or weekday). Mother-in-law worked variable represents the husband's mother's employment status when he was at the age of 14. Living arrangements are dummy variables indicating whether the couple are living with their parents. The couple's education level, the wife's occupation and her health status are a set of dummies. Region are the provincial dummies. A constant term is included in all the specifications.

* significant at 10%, ** significant at 5%, *** significant at 1%.

3.6 Robustness Checks

In this section, we conduct some robustness checks for the results obtained in Section 3.5. Firstly, we consider the possibility of potential omitted variables, since the cross-section results may suffer from endogenous concern. Specifically, we perform falsification tests using the information on women's fathers-in-law and their own mothers. The results indicate that potential omitted variables are not the main drivers of this intergenerational correlation. Secondly, we consider some alternative underlying mechanisms besides the mechanisms we have tested in Section 3.5. Specifically, we examine the potential mechanisms which are not working through mothers' influence on their sons. The results suggest the unimportance of the alternative hypotheses, which further supports the story of "mothers and sons".

3.6.1 Potential Omitted Variables

We would observe the same relationship between the working behavior of the wife and her mother-in-law due to omitted variables. It is possible that the woman who is more inclined to participate in the labor market is also more likely to choose a husband with a working mother-in-law. This could be driven by some unobserved characteristics of the wife, such as ambition and unobserved differences in skills. In other words, it is possible that the cross-sectional results are not driven by the former employment status of mother-in-law, but rather by the unobserved differences in female characteristics that happen to be correlated with the former employment status of her mother-in-law. If this is the case, it will lead to the problem of omitted variable bias and contaminate the OLS estimates.

The formation of networks always suffers the possible endogenous concern. In this case, the concern is that the unobserved factors that influence the formation of the marriage match also have impact on the women's labor market participation decision. However, it should be noted that the key variable of interest in our analysis is the working status of the husband's mother when he was 14 years old, and the dependent variable is the wife's current participation indicator. Since these two variables are not contemporary, the unobserved characteristics of the wife should be less likely to be correlated to the working behavior of her mother-in-law.

1. Women with Their Fathers-in-law

To further address this concern, we use a woman's father-in-law as a falsification test. The key variable of interest is the working status of a man's father when he was fourteen. The reasoning is that if the unobserved characteristics of a woman which affect her labor market participation decision, such as ambition, are correlated with her mother-in-law's former working status, then for the same woman, those characteristics should also be correlated with her father-in-law's working status.① Therefore, if the significant and positive correlation between the working behavior of a woman and her mother-in-law is being driven by such unobserved characteristics, then this effect should also be positive and statistically significant for her father-in-law.

Table 3.7 shows the results of the falsification test. Model (i) and model (vii) use the specifications of the baseline model and model (vii) presented in Table 3.2, only in these specifications the working status of the father-in-law substitute for the working status of the mother-in-law. In models (i)' and (vii)', we include the working status of both mother-in-law and father-in-law. In all specifications, the coefficient of the father-in-law is negative and insignificant. Interestingly, the coefficient of the mother-in-law increases from 0.162 to 0.19 using model (i)' and 0.132 to 0.166 using model (vii)' with the inclusion of the father-in-law's former work status. In addition, we use the data from the CFPS dataset to conduct the same falsification test, and gain similar results.

Table 3.7 Robustness Test: Women with Their Fathers-in-law

	(i)	(vii)	(i)'	(vii)'
Father-in-law worked	-0.0488 (0.1111)	-0.0350 (0.1383)	-0.1188 (0.1356)	-0.0937 (0.1525)
Mother-in-law worked			0.1902 *** (0.0439)	0.1660 *** (0.0459)
Husband's age	-0.0133 *** (0.0026)	-0.0105 ** (0.0052)	-0.0121 *** (0.0026)	-0.0088 * (0.0054)
Husband's income	-0.0216 (0.0232)	-0.0541 ** (0.0237)	-0.0216 (0.0226)	-0.0551 ** (0.0232)
Wife's age		0.0011 (0.0059)		0.0005 (0.0060)

---

① The underlying assumption is that no gender segregation exists, i.e. father-in-law and mother-in-law are equally helpful for the wife's career development.

continued

	(i)	(vii)	(i)'	(vii)'
Children		-0.0955 ** (0.0388)		-0.0899 ** (0.0394)
Husband's education	yes	yes	yes	yes
Wife's education		yes		yes
Husband's parents' education		yes		yes
Religion		yes		yes
Income 14		yes		yes
Region	yes	yes	yes	yes
Observations	743	716	728	704
Adjusted R-squared	0.101	0.154	0.123	0.169

Note: Robust standard errors are reported in parentheses. Linear probablity model is used for estimation. Models (i) and (vii) use the same specifications reported in Table 3.2, only the working status of the father-in-law substitute for the working status of the mother-in-law. In models (i)' and (vii)', we include the working status of both mother-in-law and father-in-law. The dependent variable is the participation indicator of the wife. Father-in-law worked variable represents the working status of a man's father when he was fourteen. Mother-in-law worked variable represents the husband's mother's employment status when he was fourteen. Religion is a set of dummies for the husband's religion. Income 14 is a set of dummies for the husband's self-assessed ranking of his family in the society when he was fourteen. Region are the provincial dummies. A constant term is included in all the specifications.

* significant at 10%, ** significant at 5%, *** significant at 1%.

2. Women with Their Own Mothers

Another way to address the concern of non-causality is to test the relationship between the working behavior of a woman and her own mother, because according to Morrill and Morrill (2013), the non-causality of this positive correlation may be due to assortative mating. Specifically, they argue that the relationship between the daughter-in-law and her mother-in-law found in Fernández, Fogli and Olivetti (2004) may be caused by the daughter-in-law's own preference formed before selecting a spouse, and her preference regarding labor force participation might actually be influenced by the former working behavior of her own mother. This alternative explanation implies the positive correlation found in the cross-sectional data could be non-causal: the women are first influenced by their own working mothers and form their preferences towards participating, then select their spouses who were also raised by working mothers.

To account for this story of "mothers and daughters", we use the sample of female respondents in the CGSS 2010. All the seven specifications in Table 3.2 have been tried and the same control variables are included, except in the models (v) – (vii), we control for the wife's own family background characteristics instead of the husband's to take alternative explanations into consideration for the reasons discussed in Section 3.4. Table 3.8 reports the results in which the estimated coefficients of a working mother are insignificant in all the seven models. [1] The insignificance of the women's own mothers' employment status is consistent with the findings of Fernández, Fogli and Olivetti (2004), and provide additional support for the causality.

Table 3.8   Robustness Test: Women with Their Own Mothers

	(i)	(ii)	(iii)	(iv)	(v)	(vi)	(vii)
Mother worked	0.0207 (0.0442)	0.0191 (0.0366)	0.0177 (0.0434)	0.0268 (0.0437)	-0.0078 (0.0465)	-0.0069 (0.0457)	-0.0002 (0.0457)
Husband's age	-0.0082 *** (0.0026)		-0.0010 (0.0057)	-0.0008 (0.0058)	-0.0086 *** (0.0028)	-0.0019 (0.0062)	-0.0022 (0.0063)
Husband's income	-0.0727 *** (0.0230)		-0.0806 *** (0.0226)	-0.0832 *** (0.0226)	-0.0928 *** (0.0245)	-0.0964 *** (0.0240)	-0.1015 *** (0.0239)
Wife's age		-0.0064 *** (0.0024)	-0.0068 (0.0063)	-0.0060 (0.0063)		-0.0065 (0.0066)	-0.0055 (0.0067)
Children				-0.0544 (0.0355)			-0.0583 (0.0386)
Husband's education	yes		yes	yes	yes	yes	yes
Wife's education		yes	yes	yes		yes	yes

---

[1] The CFPS dataset has also been used to test this hypothesis. The models (i) – (iv) yield insignificant estimates for the coefficient of the working-mother variable. However, for the models (v) – (vii), the Probit estimations of the working-mother variable are significant at 10 percent level.

continued

	(i)	(ii)	(iii)	(iv)	(v)	(vi)	(vii)
Wife's parents' education					yes	yes	yes
Religion					yes	yes	yes
Income 14					yes	yes	yes
Region	yes	yes	yes	yes	yes	yes	yes
Observations	766	1053	766	756	735	735	727
Adjusted R-squared	0.061	0.078	0.090	0.090	0.063	0.089	0.089

Note: Robust standard errors are reported in parentheses. Linear probablity model is used for estimation. Models (i) - (vii) use the same specifications reported in Table 3.2, only the working status of the wife's own mother substitute for the working status of her mother-in-law. The dependent variable is the participation indicator of the wife. Mother worked variable represents the wife's mother's employment status when she was fourteen. Religion is a set of dummies for the wife's religion. Income 14 is a set of dummies for the wife's self-assessed ranking of her family in the society when she was fourteen. Region are the provincial dummies. A constant term is included in all the specifications.

* significant at 10%, ** significant at 5%, *** significant at 1%.

3.6.2 Alternative Hypotheses

The two mechanisms we have tested so far, the preference channel and the household productivity channel, are mainly working through mothers' influence on their sons. Next, we consider some alternative hypotheses. Specifically, we investigate whether a working mother-in-law could affect the labor market participation choice of her daughter-in-law directly.

One of the potential mechanisms is that wives could receive direct assistance from their mothers-in-law regarding their labor market performances if their mothers-in-law have former working experience. The direct assistance could be in forms of, but not limited to, career advice, the skills of balancing career and family, the network, and so on. Therefore, if a woman has a working mother-in-law, she is more likely to participate. This mechanism does not work through mothers' influence on their sons, but rather focuses on the direct relationship between the wife and her mother-in-law.

If mother-in-law's impact on the wife's participation decision partially results from the fact that mother-in-law's former working experience enhanced her abilities that would be helpful to the labor market participation of the wife, those mothers-in-law in prestigious jobs should exert additional positive impact. This hypothesis is under the assumption that people in prestigious jobs could offer better career assistance. In the CGSS 2010, there is a question asking the respondent's mother's position while the respondent was 14 years old. Based on this information, we generate an indicator variable "prestigious", which equals one if the mother-in-law's position is or above "*zhengkeji*" and the mother-in-law worked while the husband was 14 years old. We include this indicator variable and re-estimate the baseline model and model (vii) in Table 3.2. In the CFPS, we generate the prestigious indicator which equals one for the mother whose education level is or beyond senior high school and was employed when the husband was fourteen. If the hypothesis is true, we should expect a positive and significant estimate for the "prestigious" indicator.

Table 3.9 shows the results. The estimates indicate that having a mother-in-law in prestigious job is not always positively correlated with the woman's labor force participation, and this effect is statistically insignificant in most of the cases. Additionally, the results gained from the CFPS show that the estimation of the prestigious indicator is insignificant in the baseline model, and even significantly negative in model (vii). Thus, the results provide some suggestive evidence that the channel of career assistance is not likely to be responsible for this positive correlation.

Table 3.9   Robustness Test: Mother-in-law with Prestigious Job

	CGSS		CFPS	
	(i)	(vii)	(i)	(vii)
Mother-in-law worked	0.1709 *** (0.0476)	0.1211 ** (0.0502)	0.0666 * (0.0342)	0.0741 ** (0.0356)

continued

	CGSS		CFPS	
	(i)	(vii)	(i)	(vii)
Prestigious	-0.0196 (0.0449)	0.0222 (0.0470)	0.0514 (0.0398)	-0.1996 *** (0.0706)
Husband's age	-0.0108 *** (0.0026)	-0.0064 (0.0053)	-0.0055 ** (0.0022)	-0.0077 (0.0047)
Husband's income	-0.0175 (0.0226)	-0.0481 ** (0.0232)	-0.0054 (0.0154)	-0.0129 (0.0156)
Wife's age		-0.0008 (0.0060)		0.0063 (0.0050)
Children		-0.0894 ** (0.0385)		-0.0386 (0.0321)
Husband's education	yes	yes	yes	yes
Wife's education		yes		yes
Husband's parents' education		yes		yes
Religion		yes		
Income 14		yes		
Region	yes	yes	yes	yes
Observations	757	729	954	924
Adjusted R-squared	0.107	0.154	0.040	0.065

Note: Robust standard errors are reported in parentheses. Linear probablity model is used for estimation. Models (i) and (vii) use the same specifications reported in Table 3.2, only adding the indicator for prestigious job. The dependent variable is the participation indicator of the wife. The indicator variable "prestigious" equals one if the mother-in-law's position is or above "*zhengkeji*" and the mother-in-law worked while the husband was fourteen. Mother-in-law worked variable represents the husband's mother's employment status when he was fourteen. Religion is a set of dummies for the husband's religion. Income 14 is a set of dummies for the husband's self-assessed ranking of his family in the society when he was fourteen. Region are the provincial dummies. A constant term is included in all the specifications.

* significant at 10%, ** significant at 5%, *** significant at 1%.

Another approach to test the potential career assistance channel is to examine the relationship of the working behavior between women and their own mothers. If the former working experience matters in regards to help with the participation for the women of the next generation, women's own mothers should have more incentive to provide such type of assistance. Accordingly, if the career assistance mechanism exists and is the major underlying mechanism, we should observe a positive and significant correlation between the current participation status of the daughter and the former employment status of her own mother. The regression results could be found in Table 3.8: the estimated coefficients of a working mother are insignificant in all the seven models. Consequently, these results render additional evidence against the potential career assistance mechanism.

Also, the results in Table 3.7 could provide some supplemental support for us to rule out this direct career assistance mechanism. Specifically, if the former working experience is directly helpful for the participation of the next generation, one could argue that the estimated coefficient of a working father-in-law should also be positive and significant. However, those estimates are insignificant. In closing, the above three evidence all indicates the unimportance of the career assistance mechanism, which further consolidates the importance of the working mothers' influence on their sons as the major mechanism underlying this positive correlation.

Another potential mechanism is that, instead of the actual career assistance in some form, it might be the case that a working mother-in-law prefers a working woman to be her daughter-in-law, and this preference could have both ex ante or ex post effect on the wife's participation status. As the career assistance channel, this mechanism also concerns with the mother-in-law's direct influence on the wife instead of through her son. However, according to our knowledge, the relevant datasets do not include information concerning mother-in-law's preference, thus we cannot directly test this potential underlying mechanism.

3.7 Conclusion

In this chapter, we find strong cross-sectional evidence showing social norms could impact the labor force participation decisions of married women. In the last section, we discuss the dynamic implications of this finding. Specifically, we propose this correlation could potentially explain part of the decline in China's female labor force participation rate during the past 30 years. As suggested in Fernández, Fogli and Olivetti (2004) and Morrill and Morrill (2013), a one-time shock in female labor force participation, such as World War II, could account for the time trend in female labor force participation through mothers' influence on their sons' gender-role preferences and household productivities. There are evidence suggesting China's state-sector restructuring during the 1990s (known as "*xiagang*") could be viewed as such one-time shock to female labor supply, as World War II for the United States, because of the certain features it possesses: during the restructuring period, women were laid off at much higher rates than men; after being laid off, women were more likely to endure longer unemployment spells than men; especially for the women with young children, if being laid off, they usually experienced greater difficulties in finding re-employment (Appleton et al., 2002; Giles, Park and Cai, 2006). The above characteristics of the reform suggest the state-sector restructuring affects women unfavorably, particularly mothers of young children, and results in serious deterioration in their employment status. Therefore, this event could be considered as a one-time shock to female employment status and would lead to a decline in female labor supply in future generations based on our cross-sectional evidence of the "mothers and sons" story. However, due to the limitations of the data available and the relative short time period after this labor market reform, we do not have sufficient information to test this hypothesis at present and will explore it in future research.

Chapter 4

Impact of Rural-to-Urban Migration on Labor Market Conditions of Urban Residents in China

    This chapter aims to evaluate the exact labor market consequence of rural-to-urban migration in China since the early 1990s. According to Meng et al. (2013), there is a remarkable increase in the number of migrant workers in cities since the mid-1990s, from around 39 million in 1997 to 145 million by 2009. This chapter intends to explore how does this important economic event affect the labor market conditions of urban residents. Specifically, I estimate the possible employment and earnings displacement effects of rural-to-urban migration on urban residents by exploiting regional variation in the rural migrant share of education-experience cells. I use multiple sets of instrumental variable to address the potential endogeneity problems associated with the rural migrant ratio in a city. The estimation results are consistent with the predictions of the textbook model of a competitive labor market, indicating the inflow of rural migrants reduces the wage and labor supply of competing urban residents.

4.1 Introduction

    Urban China has witnessed many major economic reforms since the mid-

1990s. The sharp increase in rural-to-urban migration is one of them. In 1997, the number of migrant workers in cities was estimated to be around 39 million, while this number has increased to 145 million by 2009. In the meantime, the labor force participation rate of urban residents has been declining dramatically. Before the late 1980s, the government typically assigned a lifetime job to each new entrant to the labor market who was able-bodied, so both male and female labor force participation rates in urban China were almost universal at that time, while in more recent years, labor force participation rate has dropped to around 75%. The decline in labor market attachment is especially spectacular for younger less educated people and older less educated females (Feng et al., 2012). Since rural migrants are generally of lower average education than urban residents, it has been argued that the massive rural-to-urban migration severely worsened the labor market conditions for urban residents and may partially account for this sharp decline in urban residents' labor supply. Nevertheless, still there is very limited literature empirically estimating the impact of rural migrant inflow on the labor market outcomes of urban residents, and it becomes the objective of the study.

In particular, this chapter aims to estimate the possible employment and earnings displacement effects of rural-to-urban migration on urban residents. The empirical strategy used in this study is the skill cells approach at the local level, which is to exploit regional variation in the rural migrant share of education-experience cells. In addition, to address the potential endogeneity problems associated with the rural migrant ratio in a city and to further identify the causal effects of rural migrants on local economies, I construct two sets of instruments, the lagged migrant ratio and the predicted migrant ratio, and implement instrumental variable strategy. The empirical analysis has been conducted at both provincial level and individual level using the data of the 2000 and the 2005 Census. Our estimation results indicate the presence of both employment and earnings displacement effects in urban China, suggesting the inflow of rural migrants reduces the labor supply and wages of competing urban residents.

Chapter 4
Impact of Rural-to-Urban Migration on Labor Market Conditions of Urban Residents in China

The study of this chapter contributes to the empirical literature on the relationship between migration and its effects on the local economies. The textbook model of a competitive labor market suggests the inflow of migrants should exert adverse impacts on the labor market conditions of competing natives. However, empirical studies in this field yield mixed and inconclusive results: one strand of the literature finds strong evidence for the presence of employment and earnings displacement effects (e. g. Borjas, 2003; Borjas et al., 2008; 2010; Smith, 2012); while another strand of literature provides the opposite evidence indicating the absence of such adverse effects by migrants (e. g. Card, 2009; Ottaviano and Peri, 2012; Manacorda et al., 2012). Most of the studies on the impact of migration are conducted using the immigration data. This paper utilizes the largest migration movements in human history, the rural-to-urban migration in China, and answers this question in a new setting. It is inspired by the seminal work of Borjas (2003), in which he points out the fact that immigration is not evenly balanced across skill groups and develops a new empirical strategy based on this supply imbalance.

This chapter makes three major contributions to the existing literature. Firstly, to my knowledge, this study is among the first to estimate the potential employment and earnings displacement effects of rural migrants by exploiting the regional variation in rural migrant ratio at skill-cell level (as captured by education and experience). While the differentiated skill-cell approach, using variation across regions, is emerging as dominant in recent literature (Lewis and Peri, 2014; Borjas, 2003; Borjas et al., 2006), the existing research on China's rural-to-urban migration either uses area approach or uses skill cell approach (Meng and Zhang, 2010). The combination of area and skill cell approach is especially suitable for the study of Chinese Economy, because China's *Hukou* System greatly reduces the mobilization of urban residents and spatial arbitrage arising from it, thereby supports the assumptions required to conduct regional analysis. Therefore, in this book, I use the skill cells approach at the local level to study the impact of rural migrant flow on local economies. Secondly, to address the potential endogeneity problem associated with the variable representing rural migrant concentration, I use two sets of instrumental variables which have not been explored in the previous studies on rural migrants. Particularly, I have tried the lagged migrant ratio and the predicted migrant share as instruments in attempting to estimate the causal effect of rural migrant inflow on the labor market outcomes of urban residents. Last but not least, this chapter utilizes the largest migration movements in human history to provide new evidence and contribute to the understanding of the old theoretical debate on the relationship between migration inflow and the labor market conditions of local residents.

The rest of the chapter is organized as follows. Section 4.2 provides an overview of China's *Hukou* System and its evolution. Section 4.3 reviews the literature on immigration and its effects on the local economies. Section 4.4 describes the conceptual framework, the empirical model, and the data used in this paper. Estimation results are reported in Section 4.5, and Section 4.6 concludes.

4.2 Historical Background

In this section, I briefly introduce China's *Hukou* System and review its evolution. Knowing the historical background of *Hukou* System can help us understand the categorization of rural migrants and urban residents in China, as well as the validity of the empirical strategies used in this paper.

China's *Hukou* System, also known as the Household Registration System, is a record system which intends to provide population statistics, identify personal status, and more importantly, to regulate population distribution in China. China's *Hukou* System is similar to the immigration system in the United States, except it imposes restrictions on internal migration instead of immigration. One of the most important features of *Hukou* System is its categorization of rural and urban residency, which artificially divides the population into two groups: agricultural population and non-agricultural population.

Chapter 4
Impact of Rural-to-Urban Migration on Labor Market Conditions of Urban Residents in China

Historically, *Hukou* System imposes strict restrictions on rural-to-urban migration, thus migration of peasants to cities was highly regulated. Starting from the early 1990s, motivated by the large earnings gap between urban and rural areas, rural workers released by the agricultural sector reform began to move to cities to explore job opportunities. But the number of rural migrants was quite small at that time because of the strict implementation of regulations. Since the mid-1990s, *Hukou* System gradually relaxed its restrictions on population mobilization. During the same period of time, China's urban labor market has undergone tremendous structural transformations (Feng et al., 2013), and it leads to huge demand for unskilled and cheap labor. As a result, the number of rural migrants in cities has increased significantly since then. According to Meng et al. (2013), in 1997 the number of migrant workers in cities was around 39 million, but by 2009, this number has increased to 145 million. The most recent report released by the National Bureau of Statistics suggests there is 274 million rural migrant workers nationwide by 2014.

Similarly, although less mentioned, *Hukou* System restricts the mobilization of urban residents across different cities as well. According to the calculation in Meng et al. (2010) based on censuses data[①], the proportion whose *hukou* is in one city but lives in another city in 1990, 2000 and 2005 is 1.37%, 6.30%, and 14.5% respectively. This ratio has been increasing over the years, but it is still quite low compared to western standards where labor are free to move across localities in many developed countries. The fact of low mobilization of urban residents in China provides supports to the main empirical strategy used in this paper, which is to exploit regional variation in the rural migrant share of skill cells. Regional analysis has always been criticized for treating a city or a metropolitan area as a closed labor market and ignoring the integration and spillovers across neighboring labor markets. For instance, Borjas (2003) and Borjas and

---

[①] The censuses data used in Meng et al. (2010) includes 1990 and 2000 censuses, and 2005 Mini-census.

Katz (2007) argue that the spatial arbitrage of mobile workers tends to equalize wages across local labor markets, thus it is important to use national level data to study the effect of immigration on wages instead of using cross-city or cross-state approach. However, *Hukou* System in China makes it harder for a urban resident to react to rural-to-urban migration by relocating, thereby provides additional support to the closed labor market assumption required for regional analysis, thus it makes China an exceptional experimental field to implement the approach of skill cells at the local level. ①

4.3 Literature Review

Due to the similarity of China's *Hukou* System and the immigration system in the United States, in this section, I focus on the literature regarding immigration and its effects on the local economies. The textbook model of a competitive labor market suggests that an inflow of immigrant should lower the wage of natives and exert adverse impact on their employment conditions. There is an extensive empirical literature on international migration attempting to explore this theoretical displacement effects of immigration on native workers, yet those studies yield mixed results. One of the most recent and comprehensive review of this research field is provided by Lewis and Peri (2014). Also, Kerr and Kerr (2011) survey the development in this field in one of the sections.

One strand of the literature demonstrates the existence of large employment and earnings displacement effects by immigration on native workers. For instance, Borjas (2003) shows that a 10 percent increase in supply of immigrants decreases wages of the competing workers by 3 to 4 percent, particularly for low-skilled natives. In this seminal paper, Borjas (2003) points out the

---

① Meng et al. (2010) also provide evidence suggesting the urban labor force outflow is unrelated to the rural migrants inflow.

Chapter 4
Impact of Rural-to-Urban Migration on Labor Market Conditions of Urban Residents in China

fact that immigration is not evenly balanced across skill groups (defined by levels of education and experience), and develops a new empirical strategy based on this fact. Particularly, he suggests to utilize this supply imbalance and estimate the effect of immigration by exploiting the variation in supply shifts brought by immigration across education-experience groups. His analysis is implemented at the national level due to the argument that natives and immigrants can easily move between cities in the United States. In this innovative study, Borjas (2003) also introduces the nested CES framework into the research in this field.

In recent years, in an attempt to explain the presence of the adverse effects of immigration on native workers, a lot of efforts have been made to estimate various elasticities of substitution using the underlying factor demand theory. For instance, the results obtained in Borjas et al. (2008, 2010), and Aydemir and Borjas (2007) show an effectively infinite elasticity and perfect substitutability between immigrants and natives of the same skill group. Recent literature also extends the analysis on displacement effects by redefining the skill groups. For instance, Smith (2012) explores the dimension of age and investigates the impact of the continuing growth of low-skilled immigration on the youth labor market. His results indicate that the increase in less educated immigrants has exerted more negative impact on the employment outcomes for native youth than for native adults. It is because of the greater elasticity of substitution between teens and immigrants, and also because teen labor supply is more elastic than adult labor supply. In this paper, the analysis is conducted at regional level for the native youth aged 16 and 17. In addition, the author uses instrumental variable strategy to overcome the potential endogeneity of immigrant flows.

Another strand of the literature finds little relationship between immigration and labor market outcomes of native workers. Card (2009) uses a cross-city research design and estimates the substitutability among different groups of workers. His results suggest small impact of immigration flows on the relative wages of U. S. natives. Particularly, using the nested CES framework, he provides empirical evidence suggesting that this absence of displacement effects is due to the imperfect substitution between immigrants and native workers within the same education groups. Ottaviano and Peri (2012) use U.S data and a production function framework to estimate the total wage effects of immigration for each native group. The results indicate that immigration had a small positive effect on average native wages and a substantial negative effect on wages of previous immigrants. Manacorda et al. (2012) use a pooled time series of British data and the multilevel CES production function approach, and reach the similar conclusion indicating the UK natives and foreign born workers are imperfect substitutes. Their results show that immigration has mainly affected the wages of immigrants, with little discernible effect on those who are native-born.

However, very limited research exists on the labor market impact of internal migration on Chinese urban residents. Meng and Zhang (2010) attempt to investigate the causal relationship between rural-to-urban migration and the labor market outcomes of the urban residents using instrumental approach. Following Boustan et al. (2007), they combine a series of lagged push and pull factors to construct instruments. In their paper, the main results have been obtained using area approach, while skill cell approach has also been implemented as a sensitivity test. Their results imply rural migrants exert modest positive or zero effects on the average employment and insignificant impact on earnings of urban residents.

In summary, the empirical analysis on the effect of immigration on labor market conditions of natives yields controversial and inconclusive results. Influential studies have reached very different conclusions in terms of the existence of the displacement effects and the degree of substitutability between natives and immigrants. In addition, in the context of China, rural migrants and urban residents share the same language skills and cultural background. Therefore, whether the theoretical displacement effects exist in urban China remains an empirical question and needs further investigation.

4.4 Empirical Analysis

4.4.1 Conceptual Framework

According to the standard labor supply-demand framework, an increase in the number of immigrants is predicted to lower the wage and employment of the natives who are close substitutes, and raise the wage and employment of the complementary native workers. It is simply because of the change in the relative supply of worker types caused by the inflow of immigrants. These theoretical predictions are short-run in nature, since the underlying assumptions include no changes in the stock of capital, no changes in the skill supply of natives, and no changes in the technology and productive structure.

The studies on the impact of immigration traditionally distinguish short-run and long-run effects of immigration. Typically, the adjustments in capital stocks, industry mixes, native skill supply, technology and output composition have been associated to the long-run responses to immigration (Lewis and Peri, 2014). In the long run, the increased profitability resulting from the lower wage will lead to the increase in capital flows, as well as the expansion of existing firms and the opening of new firms, thereby shift the labor demand curve to the right and mitigate the adverse effects of the initial labor supply shock.

The analysis of the short-run impact of immigration is central in this chapter. Although this chapter is not mainly based on structural specification, I briefly review the theoretical framework on the production and labor demand in this section to motivate the empirical work. [1] The set-up is to consider each area employs

---

[1] The theoretical framework on the impact of immigrants using the skill-cell approach has been discussed in great detail in Lewis and Peri (2014).

a production function to produce an homogeneous good by combining different production skills and physical capital. For simplification, all local economies are assumed to produce and consume the same good y, while they may have different skill supply as well as different production technology. Specifically, for area r, the production function can be represented as equation (4.1):

$$y_r = F[A_{K,r}K_r, L(A_{1,r}L_{1,r}, A_{2,r}L_{2,r}, \cdots, A_{N,r}L_{N,r})] \quad for\ r = 1, 2, \cdots, R \quad (4.1)$$

where K stands for physical capital; $A_{k,r}$ represents the productivity of physical capital in area r; L is the aggregate labor factor combining all the skill groups ($L_1, \cdots, L_n$) and their productivities ($A_1, \cdots, A_n$); $L_{n,r}$ is the amount of factor n used in the production in area r; $A_{n,r}$ is the productivity of factor n in area r. This production function implies the separability between capital and aggregate labor, which combined with the assumption of long-run mobility of capital and constant long-run returns for capital, indicates we can get the following reduced form:

$$y_i = f(A, \theta_{1,i}L_{1,i}, \theta_{2,i}L_{2,i}, \cdots, \theta_{N,i}L_{N,i}) \quad for\ i = 1, 2, \cdots, R \quad (4.2)$$

where A is a combination of parameters (the return and productivity of physical capital and total factor productivity), while the parameters θ_n represent the relative productivity of factor n. θ_n are standardized and $\sum_n \theta_n = 1$. In the competitive market, the wage to each skill is determined by the factor's marginal productivity:

$$w_{n,r} = \frac{\partial F}{\partial L_{n,r}} = f_n(A, \theta_{1,r}L_{1,r}, \theta_{2,r}L_{2,r}, \cdots, \theta_{N,r}L_{N,r}) \quad (4.3)$$

The commonly used functional form for the aggregate production function in recent studies is nested CES functions. Using the nested CES production function, equation (4.3) could be easily expressed as a function of the supply of the same skill, simple aggregators of other skill supply and a small number of parameters. Equations (4.1) – (4.3) suggest the migration-induced supply shock can affect the skill supply, thereby influence the wages and the labor supply decisions of the natives from various skill groups. The cells are usually constructed based on education attainment, age or experience level and nativity groups. Equations (4.1) – (4.3) constitute the basic theoretical framework motivating our empirical work. The nested CES approach is also the framework used to estimate elasticity parameters in many recent literature. However, since this paper mainly aims to examine the relationship between migration-induced supply shocks and the labor market outcomes of competing urban residents, the details of the theoretical framework are not described here.

4.4.2 The Empirical Model

To test the potential employment and earnings displacement effects, I try the regressions at both provincial level and individual level. The impact of rural migrants on the labor market conditions for the urban residents is identified by exploiting regional variation in the rural migrant share of education-experience cells. In addition, to further identify the causal effects of rural migrants on local economies, I use instrumental approach and construct two sets of instruments.

1. Displacement Effect

To investigate the potential displacement effects, I use the approach of skill cells at the provincial level. This approach has been adopted in my study for three main reasons: firstly, rural migrants in China are very unevenly distributed across regions compared to urban residents, thus it is very important to utilize this geographic variation of rural migrants to identify the impact of rural-to-urban migration on local economies; secondly, as explained in Section 4.2, China's *Hukou* System restricts city-to-city migration and reduces labor mobility, which to a large extent overcomes the spillover effect problem associated with area approach; lastly, since rural migrants are also distributed differently to urban residents in regards to skills (as captured by education and experience) and are known to be concentrated in some skill groups, I combine area approach with skill cell approach to fully utilize all the dimensions of variation.

(1) Provincial Level.

Regression models at the province level are mainly based on the frame-work of Borjas (2003) with a few adjustments in view of the objective of this paper. Specifically, I estimate equation (4.4) using 2000 and 2005 Census data respectively.

$$y_{ijr} = \theta p_{ijr} + s_i + x_j + q_r + s_i \times x_j + s_i \times q_r + x_j \times q_r + \epsilon_{ijr} \quad (4.4)$$

where y_{ijr} denotes the average value of a particular labor market outcome observed for the urban residents observed in province r who have education i and experience j. Specifically, I have considered two labor market outcomes in this paper: labor market participation status and log annual earnings.[①]

$$p_{ijr} = \frac{R_{ijr}}{R_{ijr} + U_{ijr}} \quad (4.5)$$

The key variable of interest p_{ijr} measures the rural migrants supply shock for the skill cell (i, j) of region r, and it is defined by equation (4.5), where R_{ijr} is the number of rural migrants in the skill-province cell (i, j, r), and U_{ijr} is the corresponding number of urban residents. p_{ijr} represents the share of the rural migrants in a particular skill-province cell. Additionally, in equation (4.4), s_i and x_j are vectors of fixed effects representing the group's education and experience level and q_r are the provincial dummies. For the interaction terms, $(s_i \times x_j)$ controls for the possibility that the impact of experience on a particular labor market outcome is different for different education groups, $(s_i \times q_r)$ and $(x_j \times q_r)$ control for the possibility that the impacts of education and experience level depend on the geographic location. The regressions are weighted by the number of people used to calculate the dependent variable. Standard errors are adjusted for clustering within education-experience-province cells.

I also estimate equation (4.6) using the pooled sample of the 2000 and 2005 Census data. The dependent variable y_{ijrt} is the mean value of the outcome

---

[①] To examine the employment displacement effects, I use the log of the labor force participation rate for urban residents as the dependent variable and the log of the rural migrant share as the key variable of interest. This specification follows Angrist and Kugler (2003).

variable of the urban residents of the skill-province cell (i, j, r) observed at time t. The key variable of interest is the rural migrant's share in the cell (i, j, r, t). Other explanatory variables include the vectors of fixed effects indicating education attainment, experience level, province, and time period of a specific cell, as well as the possible interaction terms.

$$y_{ijrt} = \theta p_{ijrt} + s_i + x_j + q_r + \pi_t + s_i \times x_j + s_i \times q_r + s_i \times \pi_t \\ + x_j \times q_r + x_j \times \pi_t + q_r \times \pi_t + \epsilon_{ijrt} \qquad (4.6)$$

(2) Individual Level.

To perform the analysis at the individual level, I estimate equation (4.7). This regression model has been used widely and is the typical specification used when estimating displacement effects at the individual level (Kerr and Kerr, 2011).

$$y_{zijrt} = \theta p_{ijrt} + \beta X_{zijrt} + q_r + \pi_t + \epsilon_{zijrt} \qquad (4.7)$$

where y_{zijrt} is the participation indicator or the natural logarithm of earnings of individual z from the skill cell (i, j) in region r and year t. X_{zijrt} includes individual characteristics such as education, experience, marital status, assessed value of his or her house, and the number of children in a family. Vectors of fixed effects for provinces and time periods are also included. The key variable of interest, p_{ijrt}, represents the rural migrants' density in the skill cell (i, j) in province r at time t. The regressions are weighted by sampling weights. The standard errors are clustered by education-experience-province cells.

2. Instrument Variable

As pointed out in many previous studies, the potential endogeneity problem associated with the location decisions of the migrants tends to mitigate the displacement effects. Studies have shown that local labor market conditions are very important factors attracting and selecting rural migrants, since the economic conditions is always a major motivation for migration (Clark et al., 2007). It implies that the Ordinary Least Squares (OLS) estimates may suffer from the potential endogeneity problem arising of simultaneity. Specifically, if the proposed displacement effects do exist, it is possible that we would not observe this negative partial correlation between "native" labor market outcome variable and migration density from the simple OLS estimates, because rural migrants tend to settle in the provinces with better local labor market conditions. In other words, the OLS estimates of θ would be biased towards zero. To address this concern, I implement an Instrumental Variable (IV) strategy and describe the construction of the instruments in this section. I employ two sets of instruments. Both of them rely on the correlation between the current location preference of rural migrants and the geographic settlement decisions of the rural migrants in some earlier periods.

Firstly, I instrument the current rural migrant concentration with the lagged rural migrant shares in the cell (i, j, r). The lagged ratio is a typical type of instrument used in the previous studies (Altonji and Card, 1991; Card, 2001; Cortes, 2008), and it is assumed to be highly correlated with the current rural migrant ratio but has no direct influence on the current labor market outcomes for urban residents. Since I only employ two waves of Census data in this study, I use the lagged ratio from 2000 as an instrument for the density of rural migrants in 2005. This instrumental variable is calculated at the level of province-education-experience cell.

Alternatively, I adopt the "shift-share" type instrument to supplement the analysis (Lewis and Peri, 2014). The "shift-share" formulation is another widely-used instrument for demand shocks, which was pioneered by David Card (2001). Basically, this approach predicts flows of immigration based on the lagged locations of similar immigrants, and calculates it using the information on preexisting settlements and current aggregate inflow by source province. In particular, it utilizes the fact that a rural migrant of skill cell (i, j) from province "r" is more likely to settle in province "s" if in province "s" in the earlier periods, there is a large size of rural migrants in that skill cell who are also from province "r". In China, many studies show that the past rural migrant community stocks from a source region is highly correlated with the size of the future rural migrants from the same origin (Meng, 2000; de Brauw and Giles, 2008). This might be driven by the fact that rural migrants in urban China rely heavily on informal network. Therefore, I use the interaction of the rural migrant flow from a specific source province in 2005 and the information on past rural migrant stocks in 2000 to predict the rural migrants flows in the cell (i, j, s) in the year 2005, and then use this predicted rural migrants inflow to instrument for the observed local rural migrants inflow. Particularly, I use equation (4.8) to predict the rural migrants inflow of the skill cell (i, j) in province "s" in the year 2005:

$$\hat{R}_{ijs} = \sum_{r} (Lag\_sh^s_{ijr} \times R_{ijr}) \qquad (4.8)$$

where $Lag\_sh^s_{ijr} = \dfrac{K^s_{ijr}}{K_{ijr}}$ is the share of the stock of rural migrants of the skill cell (i, j) from source province "r" who were living in province "s" in the year 2000, and R_{ijr} is the aggregate flow of rural migrants in the skill cell (i, j) from source province "r" in the year 2005. $Lag\_sh^s_{ijr} \times R_{ijr}$ is therefore the predicted value of the rural migrants of the skill cell (i, j) from source province "r" who are choosing to settle in province "s" in the year 2005, and the sum of the predicted rural migrant flows from all the source provinces ($r = 1, 2, ..., 31$) represents the predicted rural migrant inflow in the province "s" in the year 2005. Therefore, I use the predicted value of R_{ijs}, the "imputed" inflow of rural migrants in the skill-province cell (i, j, s) in 2005, as the second instrument for the actual inflow of rural migrants in the cell (i, j, s).

4.4.3 Data

The main data source used in this chapter are the 2000 and the 2005 Mini Population Censuses of China, which were collected by the National Bureau of Statistics of China (NBS). Censuses microdata are the most appropriate data source to evaluate the labor market consequence of rural-to-urban migration because of its broad coverage. I need the sample to be representative of the Chinese population in order to construct the key variable of interest-the share of rural migrants in a province for a specific education-experience group.

As discussed in previous section, this chapter estimates the possible employment and earnings displacement effects by exploiting regional variation in the rural migrant share of skill cells. Different definitions of skill cells are being explored, but the main results are obtained by defining the skill cell in terms of education attainment and potential experience. Specifically, individuals are categorized into three education groups ($i = 1, ..., 3$): persons who are high school dropouts, persons who are high school graduates and persons with some college and above; while in regards to experience, I classify the sample into 8 groups based on the potential experience with 5-year intervals ($j = 1, ..., 8$): $1-5$ years of experience, $6-10$ years of experience, and so on. Potential experience is calculated as the years elapsed since the person completed his or her education. This measure of experience is more accurate for men, but may be imprecise for women. Therefore, I try other definitions of the skill cell as robustness checks. The main results are robust to other definitions of the skill cell as well.

A person is defined as a rural migrant if he or she holds an agriculture *hukou* but is observed at urban site. A urban resident is the one with urban registration and observed at urban areas. The sample is restricted to be men aged 16 to 60 and women aged 16 to 55, with $1-40$ years of potential experience. I exclude the individuals with no valid information on the current household registration status. Also, since my analysis focuses on how does rural-to-urban migration affect the labor market conditions of urban residents, I restrict the sample to include the persons who are observed in urban area.

I generate an participation indicator for each individual in the sample which equals one if the individual is currently employed or non-employed but actively searching for jobs, and zero otherwise. The key variable of interest, the rural migrant ratio in a city, is constructed at the province-education-experience level based on equation (4.5). In addition, to address the problem associated with endogenous location decisions by rural migrants, I also tried two sets of instrumental variables. The instrument variables are calculated at the province-education-experience level as well.

4.5 Estimation Results

In this section, I present the results on both employment displacement effects and earnings displacement effects using the data of the 2000 and the 2005 Census. For each effect, I provide evidence from the analysis at both provincial level and individual level. Also, I compare the results gained from female and male urban resident samples as well as the results obtained from OLS and IV approach. The estimation results indicate the existence of both employment and earnings displacement effects in urban China.

4.5.1 Employment Displacement Effects

To explore the possible employment displacement effects, I estimate equation (4.4) for the 2000 and the 2005 Census and equation (4.6) for the pooled data. As for the analysis at the individual level, equation (4.7) is estimated. The estimation results are summarized in Table 4.1 and Table 4.2 respectively.

Table 4.1   **Employment Displacement Effects**
    (Provincial Level)

	2000 Census	2005 Census			Pooled
	OLS	OLS	IV 1	IV 2	OLS
	\multicolumn{5}{c}{Female Sample}				

	2000 Census	2005 Census			Pooled
	OLS	OLS	IV 1	IV 2	OLS
log (migrant rate)	−0.0077 (0.760)	−0.0253 (0.330)	−0.3009 *** (0.005)	−0.1093 ** (0.023)	−0.0199 (0.133)
No. of observations	552	659	556	555	1 211

continued

	Male Sample				
	2000 Census	2005 Census			Pooled
	OLS	OLS	IV 1	IV 2	OLS
log (migrant rate)	0.0135 (0.386)	-0.0063 (0.540)	-0.1579 *** (0.000)	-0.0223 (0.143)	0.0086 (0.252)
No. of observations	567	672	563	562	1 239

Note: P-values are reported in parentheses. Standard errors are adjusted for clustering within education-experience-province cells. The dependent variable is the natural logarithm of labor force participation rate for a urban residents' education-experience-province group at a particular point of time. log (migrant rate) represents the log of the rural migrant share in the same education-experience-province-year group. Instrument 1 is the lagged rural migrant share and instrument 2 is the predicted rural migrant share for the same education-experience-province cell. All regression models inlude education, experience, province, and period fixed effects, as well as the possible interaction terms.

* significant at 10%, ** significant at 5%, *** significant at 1%.

Table 4.2 Employment Displacement Effects (Individual Level)

	Female Sample				
	2000 Census	2005 Census			Pooled
	OLS	OLS	IV 1	IV 2	OLS
Migrant rate	-0.1195 ** (0.041)	0.0649 (0.118)	-0.0438 (0.466)	-0.0952 (0.159)	0.0384 (0.357)
No. of observations	39 472	147 351	147 328	147 328	186 823
	Male Sample				
	2000 Census	2005 Census			Pooled
	OLS	OLS	IV 1	IV 2	OLS
Migrant rate	-0.1813 *** (0.000)	-0.0667 ** (0.035)	-0.1801 *** (0.000)	-0.1478 *** (0.000)	-0.1087 *** (0.000)
No. of observations	40 597	149 901	149 870	149 870	190 498

Note: P-values are reported in parentheses. Standard errors are adjusted for clustering within education-experience-province cells. The dependent variable is the participation indicator for a urban resident from a specific education-experience-province group at a particular point of time. "Migrant rate" measures the rural migrant share in the same education-experience-province-year group. Instrument 1 is the lagged rural migrant share and instrument 2 is the predicted rural migrant share for the same education-experience-province cell. All regression models inlude individual characteristics such as education, experience, marital status, assessed value of his or her house and the number of children in a family, as well as the vectors of fixed effects for provinces and time periods.

* significant at 10%, ** significant at 5%, *** significant at 1%.

Chapter 4
Impact of Rural-to-Urban Migration on Labor Market Conditions of Urban Residents in China

1. Provincial Level Evidence

Table 4.1 reports the results gained from provincial level analysis. The OLS estimates are negative and insignificant in most of the cases. However, after taking consideration of the potential endogeneity and using instrumental variables, the results become negative and significant, which indicates the presence of employment displacement effects and the fact that the OLS estimates may be biased upwards. Also, the IV estimates are larger in magnitude than the OLS estimates.

Particularly, for the female sample, the OLS estimates yield negative yet insignificant results, while the estimates obtained by using the first set of instrument suggest a statistically significant negative effect. Specifically, the IV estimates show that a 10% increase in the rural migrant share will lead to a 3% decrease in the female labor force participation rate of the urban residents from the same education-experience-province group, other things constant. For the male sample, similar conclusions have been reached. Specifically, the OLS estimates are insignificant, while the IV estimates indicate a 10% increase in the rural migrant share will result in a 1.6% decrease in the male labor force participation rate of the urban residents.

2. Individual Level Evidence

Table 4.2 presents the results obtained from individual level analysis. The estimates provide additional supporting evidence for the presence of employment displacement effects. For the IV analysis at the individual level, both Two-Stage Least Squares (2SLS) and IV Probit models have been implemented using two sets of instruments.

For the female sample, the estimation results indicate the endogeneity problems associated with the rural migrant ratio variable may bias the OLS estimates. In particular, as reported in the upper panel of Table 4.2, the OLS estimation gained from the 2005 Census is positive and insignificant, yet the

IV estimates turn out to be negative and significant. We observe more statistically significant results for the male sample, which suggests the inflow of rural migrants exerts very significant negative effects on the participation status of male urban residents. This employment displacement effects are robust across specifications, subsamples, and regression models used. Specifically, the OLS estimates of the pooled sample suggest a 10 percentage points increase in the rural migrant ratio decreases the man's probability of participating in the labor market by 1.09 percentage points, and this effect is significant at 0.1 percent level. The IV estimation also shows strong and significant employment displacement effects. Compared to the male sample, the employment displacement effects for the female group are less in magnitude and significance level, which might be due to the imprecise measurement of potential experience for women.

4.5.2　Earnings Displacement Effects

To examine the possible earnings displacement effects, I estimate equation (4.4) for the 2005 Census since the wage information was not reported in the 2000 Census. As for the analysis at the individual level, equation (4.7) is estimated. The estimation results are summarized in Table 4.3 and Table 4.4 respectively.

Table 4.3　　　　　Earnings Displacement Effects
(Provincial Level)

	Female Sample		
	OLS	IV 1	IV 2
Migrant rate	−0.1512 * (0.059)	−0.2128 *** (0.009)	−0.3137 *** (0.008)
No. of observations	697	692	692

continued

	Male Sample		
	OLS	IV 1	IV 2
Migrant rate	-0.0772 (0.244)	-0.3506 *** (0.000)	0.1971 (0.117)
No. of observations	741	734	734

Note: P-values are reported in parentheses. Standard errors are adjusted for clustering within education-experience-province cells. The dependent variable is the mean of log annual earnings for a urban residents' education-experience-province group at a particular point of time. "Migrant rate" represents the rural migrant share in the same education-experience-province-year group. Instrument 1 is the lagged rural migrant share and instrument 2 is the predicted rural migrant share for the same education-experience-province cell. All regression models inlude education, experience, and province fixed effects, as well as the possible interaction terms.

* significant at 10%, ** significant at 5%, *** significant at 1%.

Table 4.4   **Earnings Displacement Effects**

(Individual Level)

	Female Sample		
	OLS	IV 1	IV 2
Migrant rate	-0.0661 (0.149)	-0.0762 (0.207)	-0.0517 (0.550)
No. of observations	78 449	78 434	78 434
	Male Sample		
	OLS	IV 1	IV 2
Migrant rate	-0.1381 *** (0.002)	-0.1734 *** (0.003)	0.0447 (0.531)
No. of observations	101 218	101 198	101 198

Note: P-values are reported in parentheses. Standard errors are adjusted for clustering within education-experience-province cells. The dependent variable is the natural logarithm of earnings of a urban resident from a specific education-experience-province group at a particular point of time. "Migrant rate" measures the rural migrant share in the same education-experience-province-year group. Instrument 1 is the lagged rural migrant share and instrument 2 is the predicted rural migrant share for the same education-experience-province cell. All regression models inlude individual characteristics such as education, experience, marital status, assessed value of his or her house and the number of children in a family, as well as the vectors of fixed effects for provinces and time periods.

* significant at 10%, ** significant at 5%, *** significant at 1%.

1. Provincial Level Evidence

Table 4.3 presents the results gained from provincial level analysis. The estimation obtained using various approaches is mostly negative and significant. For both male and female sample, the earnings displacement effects are larger in magnitude and significance level after instruments have been adopted. Overall, the estimation results suggest strong earnings displacement effects of rural migrants on urban residents of the same province-education-experience group.

Particularly, for the female sample, the coefficients in the log annual earnings regression is −0.1512 using the OLS model, and are more negative (−0.2128 using IV 1 and −0.3137 using IV 2) and statistically significant using the instrumental variable approach. All the estimates are significant at 10 percent level. This implied adverse earnings impact is similar to the results gained in the section V of Borjas (2003) using the spatial correlation approach. For the male sample, the OLS estimation shows negative and insignificant effects, yet the estimation gained using IV 1 suggests a much larger and statistically significant effect of −0.3506.

2. Individual Level Evidence

Table 4.4 exhibits the results of individual level analysis. For the male sample, the estimates are mostly significant and negative, while for the female sample, we do not observe significant results even after implementing instrumental variable strategy.

In particular, for the male sample, the OLS estimation suggests a 10 percentage points increase in the rural migrant ratio of an education-experience-province group at a particular point of time is associated with 1.38 percent decrease in the annual earnings of a urban resident from the same group, and this effect is significant at 1 percent level. The IV estimates provide further support to the causal relationship between rural migrant share and the earnings of urban residents, indicating a 10 percentage points increase in the rural migrant ratio will result in 1.73 percent decrease in the annual earnings of a urban resident from the same education-experience-province group. For the female sample, although the results are not statistically significant, the p-values of the estimates are close to 10 percent level as well.

4.6 Conclusion

This chapter uses the largest migration movements in human history and provides new evidence to the old theoretical debate regarding the impact of migration inflow on the labor market conditions of local residents. Consistent with the predictions of the textbook model of a competitive labor market, our empirical results suggest the existence of earnings and employment displacement effects, that is, the inflow of rural migrants reduces the wage and labor supply of competing urban residents.

The main findings in this chapter can be potentially used to account for the drastic decline in the labor force participation rate in urban China Since the 1990s. The empirical work on the puzzling decline in labor market participation in urban China is relatively scarce. Among the existing studies, most of the attempts have been made to assess the contribution of supply-side factors which are related to the shifts in the reservation wage. For instance, the changing family structure as examined in Shen et al. (2012) and the changing child care system as proposed in Du and Dong (2010). The findings of this chapter suggest a new and complementary hypothesis indicating the possibility of explaining the decline in labor supply from a demand-side factor's perspective. Besides, the significance and magnitude of the estimated earnings and employment displacement effects also highlight the importance of properly assessing the contribution of the changing demand-side factors to this mysterious decline in labor supply.

Last but not least, since this chapter focuses on the analysis of the short-run impact of migration, it should be noted the results only provide the estimation for the partial effect of rural-to-urban migration. For instance, as mentioned in the conceptual framework, I ignore the long-run capital adjustments induced by rural-to-urban migration, and the changes in technology and productive structure throughout my analysis. Therefore, for the interpretation and policy implications of these findings, it requires a complete assessment of many other possible consequences brought about by rural-to-urban migration.

Bibliography

[1] Agüero, J. M., and Marks, M. S. Motherhood and female labor force participation: evidence from infertility shocks. *The American Economic Review*, 2008, 92 (2): 500 –504.

[2] Alesina, A., and Fuchs-Schündeln, N. Good-bye Lenin (or not?): The effect of communism on people's preferences. *The American Economic Review*, 2007, 97 (4): 1507 –1528.

[3] Altonji, J. G., and Card, D. The effects of immigration on the labor market outcomes of less-skilled natives. In *Immigration, Trade, and the Labor Market*. University of Chicago Press, 1991.

[4] Amuedo-Dorantes, C., and Grossbard, S. Cohort-level sex ratio effects on women's labor force participation. *Review of Economics of the Household*, 2007, 5 (3): 249 –278.

[5] Angrist, J. How do sex ratios affect marriage and labor markets? Evidence from America's second generation. *The Quarterly Journal of Economics*, 2002, 117 (3): 997 –1038.

[6] Angrist, J. D. Grouped-data estimation and testing in simple labor-supply models. *Journal of Econometrics*, 1991, 47 (2): 243 –266.

[7] Angrist, J. D., and Evans, W. N. Children and their parents' labor supply: Evidence from exogenous variation in family size. Technical report, National Bureau of Economic Research, 1996.

[8] Angrist, J. D., and Kugler, A. D. Protective or counter-productive? Labour market institutions and the effect of immigration on EU natives. *The Economic Journal*, 2003, 488 (113): F302 –F331.

[9] Appleton, S., Knight, J., Song, L., and Xia, Q. Labor retrenchment in China: Determinants and consequences. *China Economic Review*, 2002, 13 (2): 252–275.

[10] Aydemir, A., and Borjas, G. J. Cross-country variation in the impact of international migration: Canada, Mexico, and the United States. *Journal of the European Economic Association*, 2007, 5 (4): 663–708.

[11] Bargain, O., González, L., Keane, C., and Özcan, B. Female labor supply and divorce: New evidence from Ireland. *European Economic Review*, 2012, 56 (8): 1675–1691.

[12] Becker, G. S. *A Treatise on the Family*. Harvard University Press, 2009.

[13] Blau, F. D., and Beller, A. H. Black-white earnings over the 1970s and 1980s: Gender differences in trends. *Review of Economics and Statistics*, 1992, 74 (2): 276–286.

[14] Blau, F. D., and Kahn, L. M. Changes in the labor supply behavior of married women: 1980–2000. Technical report, National Bureau of Economic Research, 2005.

[15] Blundell, R., and MaCurdy, T. Labor supply: A review of alternative approaches. *Handbook of Labor Economics*, 1999, 3: 1559–1695.

[16] Blundell, R., MaCurdy, T., and Meghir, C. Labor supply models: unobserved heterogeneity, nonparticipation and dynamics. *Handbook of Econometrics*, 2007, 6: 4667–4775.

[17] Borjas, G. J. The relationship between wages and weekly hours of work: The role of division bias. *Journal of Human Resources*, 1980, 15 (3): 409–423.

[18] Borjas, G. J. The labor demand curve is downward sloping: Reexamining the impact of immigration on the labor market. *The Quarterly Journal of Economics*, 2003, 118 (4): 1335–1374.

[19] Borjas, G. J., Grogger, J., and Hanson, G. H. Immigration and African-American employment opportunities: The response of wages, employ-

ment, and incarceration to labor supply shocks. NBER Working Paper Series, 2006, 12518.

[20] Borjas, G. J. , Grogger, J. , and Hanson, G. H. Imperfect substitution between immigrants and natives: a reappraisal. Technical report, National Bureau of Economic Research, 2008.

[21] Borjas, G. J. , Grogger, J. , and Hanson, G. H. Immigration and the economic status of African-American men. *Economica*, 2010, 306 (77): 255 – 282.

[22] Borjas, G. J. , and Katz, L. F. The evolution of the Mexican-born workforce in the united states. In *Mexican Immigration to the United States*, University of Chicago Press, 2007: 13 – 56.

[23] Boustan, L. P. , Fishback, P. V. , and Kantor, S. The effect of internal migration on local labor markets: American cities during the great depression. *Journal of Labor Economics*, 2010, 28 (4): 719 – 746.

[24] Brandt, L. , and Holz, C. A. Spatial price differences in China: estimates and implications. *Economic Development and Cultural Change*, 2006, 55 (1): 43 – 86.

[25] Bütikofer, A. Revisiting mothers and sons preference formation and the female labor force in Switzerland. *Labour Economics*, 2013, 20: 82 – 91.

[26] Cahuc, P. *Labor Economics*. MIT Press, 2004.

[27] Campos-Vazquez, R. M. , and Velez-Grajales, R. Female labour supply and intergenerational preference formation: Evidence for Mexico. *Oxford Development Studies*, 2014, 42 (4): 553 – 569.

[28] Card, D. Immigrant inflows, native outflows, and the local labor market impacts of higher immigration. *Journal of Labor Economics*, 2001, 19 (1): 22 – 64.

[29] Card, D. Immigration and inequality. *American Economic Review*, 2009, 99 (2): 1 – 21.

[30] Charles, K. K. , Guryan, J. , and Pan, J. Sexism and women's labor market outcomes. Unpublished manuscript, Booth School of Business, Uni-

[31] Chiappori, P. A. , Fortin, B. , and Lacroix, G. Marriage market, divorce legislation, and household labor supply. *Journal of Political Economy*, 2002, 110 (1): 37 –72.

[32] Cortes, P. The effect of low-skilled immigration on us prices: Evidence from CPI data. *Journal of Political Economy*, 2008, 116 (3): 381 – 422.

[33] De Brauw, A. , and Giles, J. Migrant labor markets and the welfare of rural households in the developing world: Evidence from China. *The World Bank Economic Review*, 2018, 32 (1): 1 –18.

[34] Du, F. , and Dong, X. Women's labor force participation and childcare choices in urban China during the economic transition. The University of Winnipeg, Department of Economics.

[35] Eckstein, Z. , and Lifshitz, O. Dynamic female labor supply. *Econometrica*, 2011, 79 (6): 1675 –1726.

[36] Fairlie, R. W. An extension of the Blinder-Oaxaca decomposition technique to logit and probit models. *Journal of Economic and Social Measurement*, 2005, 30 (4): 305 –316.

[37] Farré, L. , and Vella, F. The intergenerational transmission of gender role attitudes and its implications for female labour force participation. *Economica*, 2013, 318 (80): 219 –247.

[38] Feng, S. , Hu, Y. , and Moffitt, R. Long run trends in unemployment and labor force participation in China. Technical report, National Bureau of Economic Research, 2015.

[39] Fernández, R. Women, work, and culture. *Journal of the European Economic Association*, 2007, 5 (2 –3): 305 –332.

[40] Fernández, R. Cultural change as learning: The evolution of female labor force participation over a century. *The American Economic Review*, 2013, 103 (1): 472 –500.

[41] Fernández, R. , and Fogli, A. Culture: An empirical investigation

of beliefs, work, and fertility. *American Economic Journal: Macroeconomics*, 2009 (1): 146 –177.

[42] Fernández, R., Fogli, A., and Olivetti, C. Mothers and sons: Preference formation and female labor force dynamics. *The Quarterly Journal of Economics*, 2004, 119 (4): 1249 –1299.

[43] Fortin, N. M. Gender role attitudes and the labour-market outcomes of women across OECD countries. *Oxford Review of Economic Policy*, 2005, 21 (3): 416 –438.

[44] Fortin, N. M. Gender role attitudes and women's labor market participation: Opting-out, aids, and the persistent appeal of housewifery. Unpublished Manuscript, University of British Columbia, Vancouver, 2009.

[45] Fu, S., Liao, Y., and Zhang, J. The effect of housing wealth on labor force participation: evidence from China. Available at SSRN 2735293, 2016.

[46] Ge, S., and Yang, D. T. Labor market developments in China: A neoclassical view. *China Economic Review*, 2011, 22 (4): 611 –625.

[47] Ge, S., and Yang, D. T. Changes in China's wage structure. *Journal of the European Economic Association*, 2014, 12 (2): 300 –336.

[48] Giles, J., Park, A., and Cai, F. How has economic restructuring affected China's urban workers? *The China Quarterly*, 2006, 185: 61 –95.

[49] Goldin, C., and Katz, L. F. The power of the pill: Oral contraceptives and women's career and marriage decisions. *Journal of Political Economy*, 2002, 110 (4): 730 –770.

[50] Gomulka, J., and Stern, N. The employment of married women in the United Kingdom 1970 –83. *Economica*, 1990, 226 (57): 171 –199.

[51] Greenhalgh, S. Sexual stratification: The other side of "growth with equity" in east Asia. *Population and Development Review*, 1985: 265 –314.

[52] Greenwood, J., Seshadri, A., and Yorukoglu, M. Engines of liberation. *The Review of Economic Studies*, 2005, 72 (1): 109 –133.

[53] Grossbard-Shechtman, A. A theory of allocation of time in markets

for labour and marriage. *The Economic Journal*, 1984, 376 (94): 863 – 882.

[54] Gutiérrez-Domenech, M., and Bell, B. Female labour force participation in the United Kingdom: evolving characteristics or changing behaviour? Bank of England, 2004.

[55] He, X., and Zhu, R. Fertility and female labour force participation: Causal evidence from urban China. *The Manchester School*, 2016, 84 (5): 664 – 674.

[56] Heckman, J. J. Sample selection bias as a specification error. *Econometrica: Journal of the Econometric Society*, 1979: 153 – 161.

[57] Heim, B. T. The incredible shrinking elasticities married female labor supply, 1978 – 2002. *Journal of Human Resources*, 2007, 42 (4): 881 – 918.

[58] Hwang, J. Housewife, "gold miss", and equal: The evolution of educated women's role in Asia and the US. *Journal of Population Economics*, 2016, 29 (2): 529 – 570.

[59] Jann, B. The Blinder-Oaxaca decomposition for linear regression models. *The Stata Journal*, 2008, 8 (4): 453 – 479.

[60] Jones, F. L., and Kelley, J. Decomposing differences between groups a cautionary note on measuring discrimination. *Sociological Methods & Research*, 1984, 12 (3): 323 – 343.

[61] Juhn, C. Decline of male labor market participation: The role of declining market opportunities. *The Quarterly Journal of Economics*, 1992, 107 (1): 79 – 121.

[62] Juhn, C., and Potter, S. Changes in labor force participation in the United States. *Journal of Economic Perspectives*, 2006, 20 (3): 27 – 46.

[63] Kawaguchi, D., and Miyazaki, J. Working mothers and sons preferences regarding female labor supply: direct evidence from stated preferences. *Journal of Population Economics*, 2009, 22 (1): 115 – 130.

[64] Kerr, S. P., and Kerr, W. R. Economic impacts of immigration: A survey. Technical report, National Bureau of Economic Research, 2011.

[65] Kilburn, M. R., and Datar, A. The availability of child care centers in China and its impact on child care and maternal work decisions. RAND, 2002.

[66] Killingsworth, M. R., and Heckman, J. J. Female labor supply: A survey. *Handbook of Labor Economics*, 1986 (1): 103-204.

[67] Lei, X., Strauss, J., Tian, M., and Zhao, Y. Living arrangements of the elderly in China: Evidence from the CHARLS national baseline. *China Economic Journal*, 2015, 8 (3): 191-214.

[68] Lewis, E., and Peri, G. Immigration and the economy of cities and regions. Technical Report, National Bureau of Economic Research, 2014.

[69] Li, H. Economic transition and returns to education in China. *Economics of Education Review*, 2003, 22 (3): 317-328.

[70] Li, H., and Zax, J. S. Labor supply in urban China. *Journal of Comparative Economics*, 2003, 31 (4): 795-817.

[71] Luo, C., Li, S., Sicular, T., Deng, Q., and Yue, X. The 2007 household surveys: Sampling methods and data description.

[72] Manacorda, M., Manning, A., and Wadsworth, J. The impact of immigration on the structure of wages: theory and evidence from Britain. *Journal of the European Economic Association*, 2012, 10 (1): 120-151.

[73] Maurer-Fazio, M., Connelly, R., Chen, L., and Tang, L. Childcare, eldercare, and labor force participation of married women in urban China, 1982-2000. *Journal of Human Resources*, 2011, 46 (2): 261-294.

[74] Meng, X. *Labour Market Reform in China*. Cambridge University Press, 2000.

[75] Meng, X., Shen, K., and Xue, S. Economic reform, education expansion, and earnings inequality for urban males in China, 1988-2009. *Journal of Comparative Economics*, 2013, 41 (1): 227-244.

[76] Meng, X., and Zhang, D. Labour market impact of large scale internal migration on Chinese urban "native" workers. Technical Report, Institute for the Study of Labor (IZA), 2010.

[77] Mincer, J. Labor force participation of married women: A study of labor supply. In *Aspects of Labor Economics*. Princeton University Press, 1962.

[78] Mincer, J. Intercountry comparisons of labor force trends and of related developments: an overview. *Journal of Labor Economics*, 1985 (S1 – S32).

[79] Moffitt, R. A. The reversal of the employment-population ratio in the 2000s: facts and explanations. *Brookings Papers on Economic Activity* 2012, 2012, 2: 201 – 264.

[80] Morrill, M. S., and Morrill, T. Intergenerational links in female labor force participation. *Labour Economics*, 2013 (20): 38 – 47.

[81] Nunn, N., Alesina, A., and Giuliano, P. On the origins of gender roles: Women and the plough. *Quarterly Journal of Economics*, 2013, 128 (2): 469 – 530.

[82] Ogawa, N., and Ermisch, J. F. Family structure, home time demands, and the employment patterns of Japanese married women. *Journal of Labor Economics*, 1996, 14 (4): 677 – 702.

[83] Olivetti, C., Patacchini, E., and Zenou, Y. Mothers, friends and gender identity. Technical Report, National Bureau of Economic Research, 2013.

[84] Ottaviano, G. I., and Peri, G. Rethinking the effect of immigration on wages. *Journal of the European Economic Association*, 2012, 10 (1): 152 – 197.

[85] Parsons, D. O. The decline in male labor force participation. *Journal of Political Economy*, 1980, 88 (1): 117 – 134.

[86] Sasaki, M. The causal effect of family structure on labor force participation among Japanese married women. *Journal of Human Resources*, 2002: 429 – 440.

[87] Shen, K., Zhang, Y., and Yan, P. Family structure and female labor force participation in China. *Population Research*, 2012, 36 (5): 15 – 27.

[88] Smith, C. L. The impact of low-skilled immigration on the youth labor

market. *Journal of Labor Economics*, 2012, 30 (1): 55 –89.

[89] Vella, F. Gender roles and human capital investment: The relationship between traditional attitudes and female labour market performance. *Economica*, 1994: 191 –211.

[90] Xie, Y. Gender and family in contemporary China. *Population Studies Center Research Report*, 2013.

[91] Yao, X., and Tan, L. Family income and labor force participation of married women in unban China (In Chinese). *Economic Research Journal*, 2005 (7).

[92] Zhang, Y. J. Culture, institutions, and the gender gap in competitive inclination: Evidence from the communist experiment in China. *The Economic Journal*, 2019, 617 (129): 509 –552.

Acknowledgments

This book was written based on my doctoral dissertation. First of all, I would like to express my deepest gratitude to my advisor, Dr. Suqin Ge. Without her guidance, encouragement and patience, it would have been impossible for me to complete this book. I am truly fortunate to have the opportunity to work with her and become friends with her. Throughout my Ph. D. studies at Virginia Tech, I was led by Dr. Ge in every step, all the way from when I was first considering applying to the Ph. D. program through to the completion of this degree and the job search process. I especially thank her for her inspirational suggestions and comments on my research work. Her earnest, diligent and optimistic attitude will surely have long-lasting impacts on my life.

I would like to thank my dissertation committee: Dr. Richard Ashley, Dr. Djavad Salehi-Isfahani and Dr. Kwok Ping Tsang for their thought-provoking suggestions on my research. I also greatly appreciate for their substantial help with my job search. I am grateful for Dr. Richard Ashley's insightful comments on the econometric techniques used in my research, as well as Dr. Djavad Salehi-Isfahani cultivating my interest in development economics and giving me many practical advices on my job search. I thank Dr. Kwok Ping Tsang for reading and commenting my papers and always being there to listen and give advice, even during his sabbatical. I am also grateful to Dr. Sudipta Sarangi for the job hunting advice and his help with my interview preparation. My thanks also go to Will Bebout, Amy Stanford and Lynn Rader for all the time they have devoted to my job search and their continued support throughout my Ph. D. studies in the department of economics at Virginia Tech.

I also would like to thank Dr. Jason Taylor for offering me the graduate research assistantship to support my master's study in economics at Central Michigan University in the first place. I am also grateful for his continued care and support after I graduated. None of this would have been possible without his confidence in me. I also want to thank my dear friends and fellow doctoral students for their support, feedback, and friendship. Special thanks to Ying Xu, Yuan Zhang, Yifan Zhang, Man Zhang, Mckeon Evelyn, Lois Ingles, Tsung-Han Yang, Syed Asif Ehsan, Omid Bagheri, Poulomi Dasgupta, Mohammad Mostafavi, Atieh Vahidmanesh, Yu Zhou, Tiefeng Qian, Xiaojin Sun and Yonghui Zhang for their warm care, generous help and wonderful memories. I greatly cherish their friendship and I truly appreciate their belief in me.

I would like to extend my sincere thanks and appreciation to the School of Economics at Huazhong University of Science and Technology, especially Ms. Juan Zhang, for the help provided during the book publishing process. Thank you to editors Lili Sun and Xiaoxiao Ji for their efforts in the successful publication of this book.

Most importantly, I would like to express my sincere gratitude to my parents for their unconditional support to every decision I make. They have been always there for me, standing by my side when times get hard. I would also like to extend my heart-felt gratitude to my parents-in-law for their continuous support, concern and encouragement. I am also very thankful to my grandparents for always believing in me. The very last gratitude belongs to my husband for his persistent encouragement, love and patience. His unwavering belief in me has been a driving force behind my personal and professional growth, and his support has given me the strength to overcome any obstacle that comes my way. I feel so blessed to have met him in this small town on the first day of my Ph. D. study and I will always be grateful for that.